ALSO BY GEORGE VECSEY

Troublemaker (with Harry Wu)

Get to the Heart (with Barbara Mandrell)

A Year in the Sun

Martina (with Martina Navratilova)

Sweet Dreams (with Leonore Fleischer)

*Five O'Clock Comes Early: A Young Man's Battle
with Alcoholism* (with Bob Welch)

Kentucky: A Celebration of American Life (with Jacques Lowe)

*Getting Off the Ground: The Pioneers of Aviation Speak
for Themselves*

Loretta Lynn: Coal Miner's Daughter (with Loretta Lynn)

One Sunset a Week: The Story of a Coal Miner

The Way It Was: Great Sports Events from the Past (editor)

*Joy in Mudville: Being a Complete Account of the
Unparalleled History of the New York Mets*

Naked Came the Stranger (1/25 authorship)

BASEBALL

GEORGE VECSEY

BASEBALL

A HISTORY OF AMERICA'S
FAVORITE GAME

A MODERN LIBRARY CHRONICLES BOOK
THE MODERN LIBRARY
NEW YORK

2006 Modern Library Edition

Copyright © 2006 by George Vecsey

Published in the United States by Modern Library, an imprint of
The Random House Publishing Group, a division of
Random House, Inc., New York.

MODERN LIBRARY and the TORCHBEARER Design are registered trademarks
of Random House, Inc.

LIBRARY OF CONGRESS CATALOGING-IN-PUBLICATION DATA
Vecsey, George.
Baseball : a history of America's favorite game / George Vecsey.—
Modern Library ed.
p. cm. — (Modern Library chronicles book ; 25)
Includes bibliographical references and index.
ISBN 0-679-64338-9
1. Baseball—United States—History. I. Title. II. Series:
Modern Library chronicles ; 25.
GV863.A1V43 2006
796.3570973—dc22   2006045033

Printed in the United States of America on acid-free paper

www.modernlibrary.com

2 4 6 8 9 7 5 3 1

First Edition

To the rookies:
George
Isabel
Anjali
Elizabeth
Margaret

CONTENTS

Prologue

It's all in the mind.

—George Harrison
in *Yellow Submarine*

When we were young, we played ball in the family backyard in a quiet corner of Queens, pretending we were Jackie Robinson or Stan Musial. There was a cinder-block wall behind our house, which made it easy to imagine we were taking potshots at the concave right field wall in Ebbets Field, a few miles to our west. Occasionally, we would break a window in our neighbor's house—a tinkling sound unlike the concussion of a Duke Snider drive off the wall in Brooklyn. It was not hard to imagine the bright blue scripted "Dodgers" across our chests.

Some nights when my father was not working at his newspaper job, we would sit on camp chairs on the lawn and listen to the Dodger game, the austere voice of Red Barber and the mellifluous tones of Connie Desmond. I remember three things about those nights: how nice it was to have my father home, the rude shock when I plugged the radio into the garage socket, and the fireflies floating around at dusk. There are no fireflies like that anymore. No Brooklyn Dodgers, either.

—

Baseball with your dad. The American verity.

Half a century later, I found myself on a front lawn somewhere out in America, pitching a Wiffle Ball to my grandson.

"Hands back," I told the boy. "Turn your hip to me. Look over your shoulder at the ball."

Over the years, I have discovered the best way to teach children to hit is turning them into the twisted stance of Stanley Frank Musial, the laughing cavalier of the St. Louis Cardinals, who played his last game back in 1963.

Children are always surprised when they uncoil from the Musial stance, hitting the ball harder than they had expected. Sooner or later, their bodies will find their natural stance, but turning them into a human corkscrew is a good way to start.

The boy had already been taught well by his father, but I could not resist adding a refinement.

"And smile. Always smile. Hitting is fun," I said. Children love getting permission to whack away at something. Smiling erases anxiety, releases positive energy.

"Stan Musial always smiled," I added.

This was an exaggeration, of course. Musial only smiled after he slid into second base, raising a puff of white dust and brown dirt. I can still see Musial, his full grin lighting up the old bandbox in Brooklyn, a place he terrorized.

My grandson had never heard of Stan Musial, had no idea he was one of the great hitters of the 1940s and 1950s. All the boy knew was that his grandfather was tossing a hollow plastic ball to him on the lawn, showing him a coiled stance that worked, somehow.

Someday, if I have time, I will tell him stories that old people know about baseball, how Musial's teammate Enos (Country) Slaughter dashed home with the winning run in that wonderful World Series of 1946, and how Musial used to play the harmonica for his Cardinal teammates during long train rides—yes, train rides—and how forty years after retirement Musial would still whip out his harmonica and entertain fans outside the steamy ballpark a few blocks from the roiling Mississippi. I have seen that.

"They loved him, even in Brooklyn," I said, invoking the holy borough of my childhood team, the long-departed Dodgers. Someday I will drive my grandson past the block where we used to chase

Jackie Robinson for autographs, outside an old ballpark that is as real to me as an amputated limb might be.

"Dodger fans loved Musial even when he beat them," I said. "You know what they used to call him?"

The boy shook his head.

"Stan the Man."

My grandson smiled at the nickname, twisted into the new stance. There was still time for a few more swings before it got dark.

I

SIX DEGREES

In 1958, the St. Louis Cardinals made a barnstorming trip to Japan on the golden anniversary of the first visit by two major league squads. Among the Cardinals' entourage was Stan Musial, about to turn thirty-eight, old by baseball standards, but still exhibiting his characteristic smile and convoluted batting stance.

In the city of Tokyo was a seventeen-year-old prospect named Sadaharu Oh, the son of a Chinese noodle shop operator and a Japanese mother. Oh was already Japan's best-known high school player. His batting coach, Tetsuharu Kawakami, strongly suggested that Oh adapt Musial's coiled stance. "Hitting is with your hip, not with your hand," said Kawakami, who had won five batting titles in Japan.

With the obstinacy of a seventeen-year-old, Oh declined. Several years later, on the brink of failure that was partially self-induced through his excesses and hardheadedness, Oh would submit to his guru. With the hope of salvaging his career, Oh would accept an even more idiosyncratic posture—"the flamingo stance," the Japanese would call it. He would raise his front leg, the right one, forcing his weight and power to his back foot. The new stance had its roots in the twisted Musial position.

That earnest trip in 1958 was regarded as something of a failure by Musial, who hit only two home runs for the adoring Japanese fans. "I was tired, worn out after the regular season," Musial would recall thirty years later. "I'm sorry they couldn't have seen me earlier." Yet the trip by the Cardinals would help produce the greatest home run hitter in the history of baseball, as Sadaharu Oh would eventually hit 868 home runs.

Years later, Musial and Oh would meet, shake hands, and bow to each other, left-handed sluggers from opposite shores, comrades in unorthodoxy.

This is the beauty of baseball. Everything is connected, either by statistic or anecdote or theory or history or the infallible memory of a fan who was there, who saw it, who can look it up. It is possible to sit in the ballpark (not the stadium, not the arena, but the ballpark, a homey title claimed only by baseball) and, during the process of one game, watch several overlapping games, overlapping generations and histories, all at once. The grandson, if he is not looking around for the hot dog vendor, may see Ichiro Suzuki slap a double into the corner. The grandfather may be thinking of how Stan Musial used to smack doubles just like that.

———

The American playwright John Guare is known for his enduring play *Six Degrees of Separation,* based on a theory that there are no more than six layers between any two people on the planet. Guare was not talking about baseball, but he could have been. The so-called American game has existed in a straight and highly detectable line since the 1840s—and backward into earlier times on other continents.

The game is perpetuated in raucous living museums, many of them in the center of cities, on a continent just beginning to have some history to it. Some cities have been playing other cities for a long time now, by American standards. These old places contain triumphs and resentments, nowhere near the rivalries of the old city-states of Europe, but the beginning of history, at the very least.

The hearts of the fans contain memories of something horrible that happened in 1908, or 1940, or maybe even last week. No other American sport has so many ancient joys and sorrows. It sounds overbearingly cutesy when sportswriters in Boston refer to the Red Sox as Ye Olde Towne Team, yet in that marvelous October of 2004 the Sox labored under a cloud of communal frustration dating back to 1918 when Babe Ruth pitched the Sox to a championship, and was soon sold to the New York Yankees. When the Sox went on their memorable eight-game romp in 2004, you could hear the brass band of a century earlier: a local rock group had resurrected "Tessie," the anthem of the very first World Series of 1903. Baseball's history echoed in vibrant Fenway Park as well as the crooked streets and anarchic traffic of Boston.

Baseball fans know these links, discuss them in dens and bars and playgrounds and even at contemporary ballparks—that is, when they can be heard above the god-awful din of the modern sound system. These memories are much more than trivia or statistics; they are a way of keeping history alive.

The sport has a timeless feel to it, as if it has always been here. That is because each game is unfettered by the tyranny of a stopwatch, as anybody will attest who has ever held car keys in hand, poised in an exit portal, only to witness a nine-inning game suddenly lurch into extra innings. I am thinking here of a marathon I once covered as a young reporter in 1962, the first year of Casey Stengel's Amazing Mets, who very quickly established themselves as the Worst Team in the History of Baseball, capital letters and all. On a chilly spring night, the Mets played the equally wretched Chicago Cubs in extra innings. The game seemed interminable—refreshment stands were closed down, children were fast asleep on their parents' laps, and fans were beginning to dread getting up for work in the morning. As I sat in the stands to savor the mood of this horrendous new team so gloriously born in New York, I heard one fan say to another, "I hate to go—but I hate to stay." Those words seemed to sum up the morbid compulsion that keeps fans in their seats, quite unable to leave this silly game.

The absence of a clock is matched by the perfection of the calendar. The season begins in the hopefulness of early spring and it flourishes in the heat of the summer and then it breaks hearts in the nippy evenings of late October.

Plus, they play it every day. No other sport in the world can match baseball for constant adventures, new results. All around the world, at every moment, there are compelling sports events, many of them presented on multiple television channels—soccer goals rocketing into the net in Rio, basketballs dunked in Shanghai, nifty putts in Madrid, dazzling backhands in Melbourne, gaudy touchdowns in Dallas, vehicles whizzing across finish lines in Monte Carlo or Daytona. But only baseball summons the same cast of characters to return, a few hours after the end of the previous game.

"Let's play two," chirped Ernie Banks of the Cubs, who had often played two or even three games a day in the Negro Leagues and became an icon in the major leagues for his celebration of the daily ritual.

No other sport has this endurance. American football players must go back into their bunkers to receive six days of drills before their bodies heal enough to play again. Likewise, basketball, soccer, and hockey players cannot play every day. Yet barring injuries, baseball regulars are expected to start in 140 or 150 games out of a total of 162, with starting pitchers expected to throw once every five days.

The result of this regularity is a delightful soap opera that airs virtually seven days a week. The player who muffed a fly ball last night or stole a base or made an incredible catch must go back out there today, in front of fans who reward him or revile him for events only a few hours old.

These daily games seep into the consciousness of citizens who insist they have stopped paying attention to baseball. People say they became disillusioned at their favorite team's defection to another town or the serial labor shutdowns of the past generation, and they claim they would rather watch pro football or stock cars going around in circles, or whatever. They declare they are turned off by high salaries as well as the steroid generation that saw bulked-up sluggers whacking home runs at an unprecedented rate, but the reality is that baseball has survived gambling plots, outlaw leagues, racial segregation, depressions, world wars, the early death of a stunning number of its heroes, financial failures of teams, inept ownerships, the bad taste of its sponsors and networks, blundering commissioners, inroads by other sports. It endures.

———

Stan Musial is a perfect example of baseball's great depth of living genealogy. In recent years, Musial's radiant excellence has been squeezed by the reverence for Babe Ruth as well as Musial's two more mystical contemporaries, Joe DiMaggio and Ted Williams, and Musial has also been somewhat obscured by the great outfielders who came along in his wake—Willie Mays, Mickey Mantle, Henry Aaron, Frank Robinson, Roberto Clemente.

Yet for fans of the 1940s and 1950s, Stan Musial was a beloved figure who played 22 seasons and batted .331, a high success ratio in a sport that acknowledges daily failure. He was of average size for his generation—six feet tall, a supple 175 pounds, and more inclined to grin than to glower. Stanley Frank Musial was a child of his times, straight out of the great American Depression. His father, Lukasz, a Polish immigrant, had worked in the zinc mines in Donora, Pennsylvania, in the worst days of the murderous smog of the Ohio River valley, grateful to be working in the aftermath of the great stock market collapse of 1929. Lukasz wanted his son to attend college but the boy insisted on signing with the massive minor league system of the St. Louis Cardinals. His career, his life, would touch a century of American history.

- Baseball was never more the national game than when these desperate young men, bound to the Cardinals by a Supreme Court–endorsed reserve clause contract, played survival-of-the-fittest games. Branch Rickey, perhaps baseball's most creative executive, had salted away hundreds of Depression-era youths in tiny rural towns, in his so-called farm system. These migrant workers in frayed hand-me-down flannel uniforms were the equivalent of the Joads in Steinbeck's *The Grapes of Wrath*, although a few actually made it to the majors. The upward mobility of American youth—an athlete in the purest, most unthreatening form—has always been part of American mythology. Even in the worst moments of the Depression, people sought cheap entertainment at the movies, or the local ballpark. Family farms were failing but Branch Rickey's farms were thriving.

- Young Musial became just another body, a sore-armed pitcher due to be replaced by some other eager recruit. But his minor league manager, Dickie Kerr, had seen him swing a bat. Kerr knew a thing or two about this game. In the 1919 World Series, Kerr had won two games while some of his fabled Chicago

White Sox teammates had mysteriously under-performed as part of an odious gambling scandal. Revered as a symbol of honesty, yet working in the low minor leagues, Kerr converted Musial from a failing pitcher to a promising slugger. In Kerr's later years, Musial would buy him a house, to repay him for his encouragement.

• Joining the Cardinals' major league team late in 1941, Musial would eventually match a retired gent named George Sisler as the greatest left-handed hitter ever to represent St. Louis. Sisler, who had been discovered by Branch Rickey at the University of Michigan, had played for the other team in St. Louis, the Browns, who would ultimately be run out of town by Musial's Cardinals.

• Musial was on the winning side against Ted Williams's Red Sox, in the 1946 World Series, when all the men, at least the lucky ones, were back from World War Two. That would be the last all-white World Series. In 1947, Rickey, by then running the Brooklyn Dodgers, would bring up Jackie Robinson, the first African-American player of the century. Because of the skill of their black players, the Dodgers would supplant the Cardinals as the premier team of the National League, and Musial would never play in another World Series.

• Musial kept slashing hits right through the 1963 season, when he retired at the age of forty-two, replaced during the next season by Louis Clark Brock, who personified the alertness and speed that had characterized the Negro Leagues. Brock would break records for stolen bases, helping the Cardinals win three pennants in the next five years. Musial, a civic treasure in gracious retirement, would giggle and say the Cardinals were winning because they finally got themselves a good left fielder.

• The first great hitter of St. Louis, George Sisler, modest and sedate, had been eclipsed by Musial and other hitters until 2004, when his record for hits in a major league season was threatened by another left-handed hitter: Ichiro Suzuki, formerly with the Orix Blue Wave of Japan. Playing for the Seattle Mariners, a team that had not existed in the time of Sisler or the time of Musial, a team owned by Japanese merchants of the electronic game Nintendo, Ichiro was the perfect ballplayer for the new age of the Pacific Rim. In that worldly city where people shop for fish and rice in Asian supermarkets, Ichiro's aura was of a master craftsman who was respected by the hometown fans, as Sisler had been in one generation, and Musial had been in another. The great players have a way of being unique, yet after fifteen decades of baseball they also have a way of fitting a pattern.

The spectacle of baseball is ancient. When settlers in America's Northeast romped through a game of town ball, an early version of baseball, they did it in close proximity to walls and windows, roofs and chimneys, flowers and gardens.

Baseball is as urban as sparring gladiators in the Colosseum, fighting each other, fighting lions, the scent of terror and failure and blood sickly-sweet in the air. Baseball is as urban as bearbaiting on the south bank of the Thames, a spectacle that competed for shillings with the words of Shakespeare and Jonson.

Nowadays in glittering and brutally noisy ballparks in the center of cities, fans scream as if life were at stake, urging pitchers to throw blazing fastballs within inches of the batters' chins. This is not some bucolic pastime, even when Willie Mays or Ken Griffey, Jr., is chasing a line drive in some downtown meadow.

In North America, baseball lives in the framework of a century of performance and legend, duly recorded. Whenever a player makes a mental mistake in a vital game, fans and broadcasters and writers (although not the players, who are rarely students of the game) still bring up the memory of poor Fred Merkle, a nineteen-year-old rookie who got a rare chance to play and helped cost the New York Giants a pennant because he neglected to step on second base. This was in 1908, mind you. Merkle's name still comes up today.

—

The game survives on its oral tradition. What else do you do at the ballpark but chatter for two or three or four hours? In rural America, people sat on their front porches and whittled with their knives and talked to each other. In ballparks, fans and players and commentators still have time to play with words and ideas and memories. Some fans debate the fine points of strategy, while others compare Babe Ruth and Barry Bonds, Ty Cobb and Pete Rose, Sadaharu Oh and Henry Aaron, Wee Willie Keeler and Ichiro Suzuki, as if they had seen them all play. Stumpy ornery Earl Weaver in Baltimore in the 1970s reminded people of nobody more than stumpy ornery John J. McGraw in Baltimore in the 1890s.

With all their free time in dugouts and bullpens and clubhouses, players still come up with new expressions for the commonplace. There are as many names for home runs as Eskimos have for snow—dingers, taters, going yard. There are words for whatever transpires after the ball is hit: Can of corn. Frozen rope. Worm-killer. Snow cone. Fans delight in eccentric names for effective pitches: Eephus. Scroogie. Lord Charles. Mister Snappy. There was even a prodigious fastball known as the Linda Ronstadt because it "Blue Bayou."

People still relish the great player nicknames of the past. A fleet, sure-handed outfielder from Brooklyn named Robert Vavasour Ferguson, who played from 1871 to 1884, was known as "Death to Flying Things," because of the way he tracked down fly balls. Superb players of the twentieth century were called the Georgia Peach, Old Reliable, Dizzy, and Shoeless Joe. Pepper Martin was the Wild Horse of the Osage. The aging fat-cat Yankees watched a brash rookie dash to first base on a walk during a lazy spring exhibition in 1963, which is how Pete Rose became known as Charlie Hustle.

Baseball lends itself to narration because it can be parsed and reconstructed, pitch by pitch, through the hieroglyphics on a scorecard—where the characters were, what they were doing, leading to speculation about what they were thinking and saying. Corny or downright inaccurate, baseball movies and baseball novels capture the national myths and history. We all know enough about baseball not to be taken in, yet we are, all over again, even when the actor has no semblance to a great athlete—Gary Cooper as Lou Gehrig? William Bendix or John Goodman as Babe Ruth? Still, put an actor in a flannel uniform and give him something formidable to ponder (a bribe offer, a fatal illness, a provocative female owner, or a literate groupie) and Americans automatically relate.

Baseball artifacts have now become collectibles, part of Americana. A turn-of-the-century Honus Wagner card or a Mickey Mantle rookie card could help finance a college education—if it is in flawless condition, not battered and scuffed from being traded and scaled against walls by children. Baseball caps, jerseys, autographs, and assorted doodads are tradable commodities today, yet in their purest form they are an indicator of the deep hold of baseball on the American psyche.

Long before all the other team sports, baseball language wafted upon the summer breeze, from open windows and street-corner debates. Games on the radio and articles in mass newspapers made the general populace familiar with the lingo of baseball, which blended into daily life: when politicians call for harsh measures in sending criminals to jail for a long time, they talk about "three strikes and out"; somebody describing a promising first date may use the phrase "getting to second base."

The game is celebrated in the song "Take Me Out to the Ball Game," particularly when bellowed by the earthy broadcaster Harry Caray, grossly shirtless, leaning out of his booth on a steamy Chicago afternoon.

The song is so pervasive in the American mind (particularly with a good old-fashioned organ accompaniment) that the government should make it part of the naturalization quiz. Even people who say they follow only golf or soccer or football secretly know the tune, to their chagrin. Paul Tagliabue, the highly effective commissioner of the National Football League—himself a jock who once led the Georgetown University basketball team in rebounding—professes to have been terminally bored by baseball as a child. But I bet if you jabbed him with truth serum even Tagliabue could sing "Take Me Out to the Ball Game," complete with the exaggerated arm waving and mugging of Harry Caray. In fact, I'd pay money to see that very serious lawyer performing the song. It's in there somewhere.

The words were written by Jack Norworth in 1908 and the music was added by Albert Von Tilzer. Norworth's words caught the feel of the game perfectly, particularly considering that he never set foot inside a ballpark until 1940, and clearly was not influenced by television, there having been no telecasts at the time. The song immediately conjures up feelings of good times, summer days, cold beers, maybe even some knowledgeable fans sitting around me, discussing the good old days.

The sport also has its epic poem, its *Beowulf,* entitled "Casey at the Bat," written by Ernest Lawrence Thayer in 1888, about a beloved slugger who had his chance to make the hometown fans happy:

> The outlook wasn't brilliant for the Mudville nine that day;
> The score stood four to two with but one inning more to play.
> And then when Cooney died at first, and Barrows did the same,
> A sickly silence fell upon the patrons of the game.

Thayer's poem, which continues for twelve more stanzas to its inevitable dismal ("There is no joy in Mudville") conclusion, has been performed at banquets for over a century, both in fact and fiction. In his delightful book *The Southpaw*—one of the very best baseball novels ever written, about a quirky lefty from upstate New York—Mark Harris depicts a sportswriter from the small hometown paper who recites "Casey at the Bat" whenever he has a few drinks in him:

> . . . I went back and found Bill standing on the seat in the car behind reciting "Casey at the Bat" whilst 2 conductors tried to coax him down like you try to coax a cat out of a tree, and I laughed and said why did they not just drag him down, and they said it was against the rules of the railroad. I said I was not under railroad rules myself . . . .

Casey's Mudville has become the symbol of all towns that dare to root for their faltering darlings. When I wrote a book about the shocking World Series victory by the formerly hideous Mets in 1969, the editor ceremoniously wrote down the title for me on a slip of paper: "Joy in Mudville." The book is long out of print; the title remains brilliant.

I could get mawkish and declare that the sport has gone to hell because of (a) money or (b) television or (c) the owners or (d) the players, but the truth is, today's players are consistent and familiar to us—our national sporting theater, our knights and louts and fallen angels, our saints and sinners, our samurai and shamans. We have known them a long, long time.

II

BERBERS WITH BATS

In 1937, seeking a tribe of Berbers rumored to have blond hair, an Italian demographer trekked the wilds of Libya. The demographer, Corrado Gini, not only located the tribe and confirmed its blond traits but also discovered that the tribesmen played a game involving a bat, a ball, and bases. Gini may not have known of the Giants' Mel Ott or the Yankees' Joe DiMaggio, who would play in the New York Subway Series that autumn, but he did recognize elements of the so-called American sport of baseball.

Gini filmed the Berbers playing the game, which they called "ta kurt om en mahag," meaning "the ball of the pilgrim's mother" in the Hamitic language. Gini later presented a scholarly paper, postulating that both the light-hair genes and the ball game had surely been brought by early Europeans, long before the Christian era. He compared the Berber game to what one historian has called "ancient spring rain rituals of the Berbers," as described by the Greek historian Herodotus 500 years before Christ.

Otherwise preoccupied with outlasting the Depression, Americans did not take notice of Gini's theory in 1937, but if they had, they would have found it somewhat inconvenient, since the young country was gearing up for a centennial celebration of baseball along with the opening of a Baseball Hall of Fame. Gini's discovery defied the American creationist myth that baseball had been invented on a certain day in 1839 in the bucolic upstate New York village of Cooperstown.

Since Gini, other historians, archaeologists, anthropologists, and social scientists have discovered incidents of bat-and-ball games in the ancient past. Eons and eons before Sandy Koufax and Bob Gibson arrived on this earth, people were throwing and hitting small objects, perhaps even scuttling from pillar to post, or base to base, if the spirit moved them. Bat-and-ball games seem to be a rather basic human pleasure, easily improvised by a couple of bored sentries or monks or schoolgirls with access to a thin stick and something round. The rules sort of fall into place.

As David Block recounts in his book *Baseball Before We Knew It: A Search for the Roots of the Game* there are ancient references to Lydians, Persians, Indians, Egyptians, Greeks, Romans, and northern Europeans, all playing one form or another of bat-and-ball games for ritual or recreation. There are wall paintings in Egyptian royal tombs and indications of Mayans playing in the Yucatán. In 1085, an early version of the game, called "stool ball," is mentioned in England's Domesday Book.

A drawing from Spain in 1251 shows people tossing a ball underhand and others hitting, holding a slightly tapered bat with a contemporary grip. The fielders are cautiously using two hands to catch the ball. "There's a bat and there's a ball," Ted Spencer, the curator of the Baseball Hall of Fame, said in 2004, long after the Doubleday mythology had been sorted out. "It looks like two guys playing baseball to me," Spencer added.

In the Walters Art Museum in Baltimore, a mile from the upscale food court and retro architectural touches of the Camden Yards stadium, is a drawing from the Ghistelles Calendar from Flanders in 1301, depicting one young man pitching to another young man, who is holding a very definite bat object with a narrow handle and a thick stock.

"Great arm extension! You can kiss that one good-bye," reads the caption in Block's book under drawings of early batting stances, the language a parody of the Mel Allens and Ernie Harwells of broadcasting, who would appear on the scene more than six centuries later.

Long before peanuts and Cracker Jacks and the seventh-inning stretch, the game of baseball underwent many changes. In 1598, John Stow's classic Survey of London described one game played in that ancient city: "After dinner all the youthes go into the fields to play at the ball. . . . The schollers of euery schoole haue their ball, or baston, in their hands: the auncient and wealthy men of the Citie come foorth on horsebacke to see the sport of the young men, and to take part in the pleasure in beholding their agilitie."

In London in 1744, John Newbery published a children's book, *A Little Pretty Pocket-Book,* which contained, according to Block, the first reference to the game, within the following poem:

> B is for Base-ball
> The Ball once struck off,
> Away flies the Boy
> To the next destin'd Post,
> And then Home with Joy.

One of the first writers ever to praise the inner qualities of baseball was a German, Johann Christoph Friedrich Gutsmuths, in his 1796 book *Games for the Exercise and Recreation of the Body and Spirit for the Youth and His Educator and All Friends of Innocent Joys of Youth.* Gutsmuths describes a game called "Ball with Free Station, or English Base-ball," in which runners can be retired in various ways including throwing the ball at them or throwing the ball to a base and shouting "Burned!"

The cataloguer also described an eighteenth-century German version of a ball game but he preferred the English version because it demanded "attentiveness"—the alertness that parents try to teach nine-year-olds on grassy Little League fields: "Think ahead! What will you do if the ball comes to you?"

Gutsmuths even goes into minute detail of the rules, including a fascination with the possibility that two runners will wind up on the same base: "This once again calls for the order of the game: there can only be one person at one base at any time."

Thus, in 1796, in the reign of Duke Carl August of Saxony-Weimar-Eisenach, Gutsmuths was projecting 130 years into the future, anticipating the base-running foibles of the Brooklyn Dodgers of the 1930s, who had a habit of clustering on one base or another. (Three men on third base was a specialty of those Dodgers, which earned them the nickname of the Daffiness Boys.)

Jane Austen describes the quotidian life of an eighteenth-century tomboy in her 1815 novel, *Northanger Abbey:* "It was not very wonderful that Catherine, who had by nature nothing heroic about her, should prefer cricket, base ball, riding on horseback, and running about the country, at the age of fourteen, to books."

In England, the bat-and-ball games evolved differently, one version branching off into cricket, with a flat bat, prevalent in southeast England, while in southwest England the ball was flipped up by a lever or catapult and became known as "One hole cat" or "One o' cat," a phrase heard in American sandlots in the late 1940s, when children still knew how to amuse themselves by playing games on their own. In another English version, two teams circled three holes or bases before heading home, giving the name to a game called "rounders."

Given the westward traffic across the Atlantic, it was inevitable that ball games would be imported to the New World. The earliest documented version was in Jamestown, Virginia, in 1609, not imported by English settlers but rather by Silesian glass-blowers. The game was called "palant" or "pilka palantowa" (bat ball) by the Silesians, who very quickly fled back to civilized Europe.

Two main forms of bat-and-ball games evolved in the New World. The recently coined phrase "Red Sox Nation" suggests the flinty old colonies waiting for the Red Sox to redeem them. A recent discovery confirms that people in New England and upstate New York played a game of town ball that was considerably different from the game of baseball developed around New York City at the same time.

Late in the twentieth century, researchers in Pittsfield, Massachusetts, stumbled on an ordinance from 1791 that banned the playing of baseball within eighty yards of the big church in the town square, an indication that bands of players of town ball were breaking windows and trampling bushes and interfering with commerce in a 360-degree version of the game.

The game that flourished around New York City was refined into two teams of approximately nine players. There are two newspaper references to baseball games in lower Manhattan, dating back to 1823. In 1840, a young doctor—Daniel Lucius Adams, born on November 1, 1814, in Mont Vernon, New Hampshire, and a graduate of Yale University and Harvard Medical School—moved to New York and began playing a version of baseball with a square of four bases, as part of the New York Base Ball Club. Doc Adams has only recently been advocated as a pioneer by the historian John Thorn.

"Some of the younger members of that club got together and formed the Knickerbocker Base Ball Club, September 24, 1845," Adams wrote later. ("Knickerbocker" was a familiar Dutch name in New York, previously named New Amsterdam.) "The players included merchants, lawyers, Union Bank clerks, insurance clerks and others who were at liberty after 3 o'clock in the afternoon. They went into it just for exercise and enjoyment, and I think they used to get a good deal more solid fun out of it than the players in the big games do nowadays," Adams added.

The modern game was codified into recognizable form in New York City around 1845 by Alexander Cartwright, a bank teller and volunteer fireman. He is given credit for the rules that called for flat bases at uniform distances, three strikes per batter, and nine players in the field. The game also produced an umpire, who at first sat at a table along the third-base line, occasionally in tails and a tall black hat. He did not call balls or strikes or even outs on the base path but served more as a mediator for group decisions involving players and even fans.

Perhaps the first big recorded game in American history took place on June 19, 1846, when the Knickerbockers took a ferry across the Hudson River to a grassy picnic grove appropriately named the Elysian Fields in Hoboken, New Jersey, where they lost to the New York Club, 23–1, with Cartwright serving as umpire.

After one game in 1858, the Knickerbockers posed for a rudimentary photograph, staring poker-faced at the newfangled camera, their bushy beards and muttonchop sideburns making them spiritual ancestors of the fightin' Oakland A's of the mid-1970s, with their retro facial hair.

Hoboken, the birthplace of another American institution, Francis Albert Sinatra, has lobbied to be considered the home place of baseball, but its urban grit and anonymous proximity to New York City make it a poor competitor with upstate Cooperstown for the honor. In the minds of the American builders of baseball, the game needed the appeal of the woods and pastures, with the players retaining the posture of farmers and outdoorsmen. This image was more myth than reality; baseball was a city game.

Within a few miles and short ferry rides, the Knickerbockers could challenge teams like the Empires, Atlantics, Eagles, Putnams, Washingtons, Gothams, Eckfords, and Phantoms in Brooklyn, Manhattan, and New Jersey, whose rosters included men from the shops, factories, offices, and civil service of the metropolis. Some clubs were organized along ethnic lines, like soccer teams of future generations, but others represented trades or companies or neighborhoods.

Cartwright did not stick around to see how it turned out. In 1849, he heard of the Gold Rush in California and headed west, with bat and ball at reach. Cartwright is often called the Johnny Appleseed of baseball for the way he carried the sport on his westward peregrination. Cartwright deserves a great deal of credit, but he was not the only pioneer.

In 1857, Doc Adams, as the head of the Knickerbockers, may have invented a defensive position known to this day as shortstop, roaming into the open space beyond second and third bases to handle relays because the ball was too light to be thrown long distances. The winner was the team that was ahead after nine innings, rather than the first team to score twenty-one runs.

Perhaps the most brilliant rule was setting the bases ninety feet apart, most notably from home to first. How did the pioneers determine that ninety feet was exactly the proper test of a pitcher, batter, infielder, and first baseman? Could they foresee generations of what are called bang-bang plays at first base, with an umpire watching the runner's foot and listening to the smack of the ball in the glove at the same time? That perfect distance has survived from rudimentary shortstops like Doc Adams of the 1850s to disparate shortstops like squat Honus Wagner early in the next century to spindly Marty (Slats) Marion of the 1940s to acrobatic Ozzie Smith of the 1980s to solid Derek Jeter and Alex Rodriguez at the turn of another century. The fielders became bigger and faster with better equipment; so did the batters racing down to first base. Unlike basketball, in which players seem to have outgrown the dimensions of the court and the basket, baseball players still succeed or fail by the same slender margins. In this way, the game remains unchanged.

Other aspects of 1850s baseball were bound to change. For a time, players were expected to remain amateur. In 1858, while Adams was active with the Knickerbockers, the players formed the National Association of Base Ball Players. They thought it was their game, although they would soon learn differently.

In that same year, an admission fee was charged for a baseball game for the first time, for an all-star game between players in New York and Brooklyn, then a separate city. Over 10,000 fans crowded into the Fashion Race Course in Queens, in what is now called Corona, not far from the current Shea Stadium. After expenses, the players donated the profits of $71.09 to help support the fire departments of the two cities, but businessmen could not help but notice that money could be made from baseball. Within the next decade, gates and turnstiles were installed and proprietors began charging a dime or a quarter to see crack touring teams like the Brooklyn Excelsiors of 1860, who traveled to Albany, Troy, Buffalo, Rochester, and Newburgh in upstate New York and on to Baltimore and Philadelphia.

By charging admission, baseball produced a higher level of competition. At first, the pitcher threw underhanded from forty-five feet, which was later moved back to the current sixty feet, six inches. The early pitchers were expected to merely lob the ball to the hitters, but the financial stakes prodded pitchers to try to blow the ball past the batter. It is reassuring to know that Roger Clemens heaves a fastball from exactly the same distance as Cy Young did— not just sixty feet but sixty feet, six inches. To speak of this distance is to recite the sacred prayer of an ancient religion, with centuries of begats.

The first gate attraction, on the order of Sandy Koufax or Fernando Valenzuela, two spiritual descendants, was James Creighton, born in 1841, who played for the Brooklyn Niagras. At seventeen, Creighton developed an underhanded hard-breaking "speedball" with a "wrist snap" and "spin" that made him "the first professional star" in the judgment of Leonard Koppett, a sage of the following century.

Creighton was also a powerful hitter. In 1862, he swung so hard while hitting a home run that he caused a fatal internal injury, perhaps a ruptured bladder, and he died at his home days later, at the age of twenty-one. His early death, mourned in many neighboring states, made him the first popular baseball player to die at an early age. That morbid list now includes Ray Chapman, killed by a pitch in 1920, Yankee heroes like Lou Gehrig and Babe Ruth along with Thurman Munson, the Yankee captain who crashed his jet plane in 1979, as well as Tony Conigliaro, whose life was shortened by a fastball to the head, and Roberto Clemente, who died in an airplane crash in 1972 while delivering goods to earthquake-stricken Nicaragua. Creighton had the dubious honor of being the first.

By the start of the Civil War, when there were already hundreds of teams in the Northeast, the game extended southward, played (separately) by white and black Southerners. Legend has it that Abraham Lincoln and his son Tad watched games behind the White House. Even in the middle of the war, baseball had its first professional free agent in A. J. Reach, who in 1864 was hired by the Philadelphia Athletics from the New York Eckfords. This was only the start of his financial prowess, for Reach established a sporting goods chain that bore his name.

In 1863, Ned Cuthbert of the Philadelphia Keystones stole a base and when ordered to return to first, he reminded the umpire that no rule prohibited him from taking off. Life promptly became tougher for catchers, who had not yet seen the wisdom of wearing glove, mask, and protective cup against increasingly hard-thrown pitches and foul tips.

The game boomed after the Civil War, supported by the relative prosperity and hopefulness of a postwar nation, particularly up North. With trains running, factories smoking, cities growing, there was space and time and money for green enclosures, for entertainment, and inevitably for sport. The Cincinnati Red Stockings of 1869 had exactly one player from the city they represented, with eight other players imported and paid for their baseball skills while allegedly making hats, selling insurance, keeping books, and building pianos to live up to the vestigial amateur pretensions of the day.

The manager, Harry Wright, an English-born son of a famous cricketer, conducted regular practices, outfitted his players in uniforms, and installed diets as well as bans on tobacco and alcohol, in theory, anyway. The star of the team and its most expensive player was Harry's brother, George Wright, who signed on from New Jersey for $1,400. In 1869, the Red Stockings barnstormed around the country, as far away as California, playing all takers, winning 65 and tying 1, and on June 26, 1869, the Red Stockings were invited to the White House, where President Ulysses S. Grant praised what he called "the western Cinderella club."

Cinderella did not thrive for long. The next season, the Red Stockings won 27 straight games but then lost to the Brooklyn Atlantics, which seemed to instantly ruin their aura. With attendance down, the first openly professional team in the United States did the truly professional thing: It relocated from Cincinnati to Boston.

In decades to come, many other cities, from Baltimore to Brooklyn, from Milwaukee to Montreal, would lose beloved teams, but Cincinnati was the first. Bottom-line economics had brought heartache and disillusionment to hometown fans. Modern baseball had arrived.

III

THE FIRST ENTREPRENEUR

Albert Goodwill Spalding, more than any other man, is responsible for baseball being America's signature sport. He started off as a pitcher but became a businessman as well as an evangelist for the sport, determined to link baseball with the American character.

A complicated man, part crass, part visionary, Spalding was a doer and a seer, not unlike Ted Turner, the American sailor and television visionary, or Richard Branson, the British balloon pilot–businessman, one century later. He detected a spiritual side to baseball much the same way other nineteenth-century men saw a higher calling in peddling cereal or coal. His blend of American capitalism and American nationalism led to his claim that baseball gave "a growing boy self-poise, and self-reliance, confidence, inoffensive and entirely proper aggressiveness" as well as "general manliness."

Spalding began his pitching career in Illinois, and was good enough to be hired by the Red Stockings when Harry Wright moved the team from Cincinnati to Boston. From 1871 through 1875, Spalding started 282 games and finished 262 in an era when pitchers were expected to finish their games. In turn, Spalding expected to be treated and paid as a professional rather than a quasi-amateur.

"I was neither ashamed of the game nor of my attachment to it," he later wrote in his 1911 book, *America's National Game*. "Mr. Wright was there offering us ... cash ... to play on the Boston team. ... Why, then, go before the public under the false pretense of being amateurs?"

The age of amateurs came to an end on St. Patrick's Day, March 17, 1871, with the formation of a new National Association of Professional Base Ball Players. Nine teams joined up—the Boston Red Stockings, Chicago White Stockings, Philadelphia Athletics, New York Mutuals, Washington Olympics, Troy (New York) Haymakers, Fort Wayne (Indiana) Kekiongas, Cleveland Forest Citys, and the Rockford (Illinois) Forest Citys. In the twenty-first century, some of these teams and cities have a decidedly minor league ring to them, but in their time they represented major metropolitan areas in the northeast quadrant of the United States, greater than war-torn Atlanta, which counted 21,789 residents in 1870, or Los Angeles, which counted 5,727, or Phoenix and Dallas, which counted no residents whatsoever.

With baseball still somewhat of a regional spectacle, Spalding became one of the most visible and popular players, but he was not satisfied with taking his turn as pitcher every couple of days. He had grander dreams. In the middle of the 1874 season, not yet twenty-four, Spalding arranged for the Boston and Philadelphia teams to barnstorm around England. Since the Boston manager, Harry Wright, and his brother, George, had grown up playing cricket, the two teams issued a challenge to play the English game as well as baseball. "We are not much in practice, but we are great in matches," Spalding was said to have bragged.

The American players demonstrated their sport in Liverpool, Manchester, London, Sheffield, Boston, and Dublin, faring better at baseball than cricket. In order to even out the cricket match, the English let the Yanks use eighteen fielders while they used the normal number of eleven. Baseball mystified most of the British, as indeed it still does. During this tour, Spalding heard people talking not only about English roots of baseball but also an old French game of "thèque," both sports akin to his.

Upon Spalding's return from England, he began a long and symbiotic relationship with a British-born journalist, Henry Chadwick, who had switched his enthusiasm from cricket to baseball after migrating to the United States. Writing in the rudimentary sports pages, Chadwick portrayed the players and also described the action in what was already the most noticeable American sport. He also fit into Spalding's mission to spread the gospel of baseball by having the players portrayed as role models for the emerging American society, in order to rid it of its leftover European identification.

Writing in *Beadle's Dime Baseball Player,* one of the early publications, Chadwick said the trip "set to rest forever the much-debated question as to whether we [have] a national game or not," while "demonstrating the character and habits of our American base ball professionals." Chadwick loved to describe how Albert Goodwill Spalding personified the American character. While Spalding was still pitching in Boston circa 1874, Chadwick described him as "intelligent and gentlemanly," a man who "both on and off the baseball field conducts himself in a manner well calculated to remove the public's bad impression as to professional ball tossers, created by swearing, gambling, specimens who form the black sheep of the flock."

Spalding showed his mercenary side in 1876 when he and three teammates left Boston to join the Chicago White Stockings in the new National League. "Boston is in mourning," said the *Worcester Spy*. "Like Rachel weeping for her children, she refuses to be comforted." In one of the first great newspaper free agent lamentations, Boston was in mourning forty-four seasons before it would lose another star pitcher, named George Herman Ruth.

Ever the innovator, as manager in 1876 and 1877, Spalding formed a reserve team that played a lesser schedule of clubs around the Chicago area, a forerunner of the farm system that Branch Rickey would implement four decades later. The reserves proved unprofitable and the excess players were traded away, but Spalding had shown his tendency to think big. He showed the same entrepreneurial side by giving away copious supplies of free tickets to Chicago's aldermen, clerks, commissioners, police officers, and even mayors, who were delighted to receive them. In his own way, he was the Bill Veeck of his time, cooperating with the newspapers, even the ones who criticized him. He once told Harmony White of the *Chicago News* that "good liberal roasts in newspapers of wide circulation are much more effective than fulsome praise." But unlike Veeck, who took pleasure in a cold beer on a Sunday afternoon, or any afternoon, Spalding held the line against Sunday games as well as selling alcohol in the ballpark.

Spalding would pitch only two more seasons because he had more important things to do—like getting rich. After seeing George and Harry Wright open a sporting goods store in New York, and

A. J. Reach manufacture baseballs and sell equipment in Philadelphia, Spalding realized there was money to be made from baseball. He concentrated on running the White Stockings while his younger brother, Walter, worked in the store, and A.G.'s mother sewed team names like "Indianapolis" across the fronts of the uniforms.

For a brief time, Chadwick criticized Spalding for jumping clubs, but by 1877 Chadwick was professing that Spalding "has sense enough to know that fair and manly play, and honorable and faithful service are at least as much the essentials of a professional ballplayer as skill in the field and at the bat." In 1884, Chadwick became the editor and spokesman for Spalding's growing collection of baseball guides and publications.

Chadwick was far more than a dutiful praise-singer. With a flair for mathematics, he devised a system of recording every single play on a scorecard and then summing them up in a box score. To this day, no other sport has the variety of statistics that intrigue fans—wild pitches, stolen bases, errors. One of Chadwick's symbols was "K" for strikeout, on the theory that K was "the prominent letter of the word strike, as far as remembering the word was concerned." When today's fans hang a series of K banners over the grandstand railing to denote a strikeout by the hometown fastballer, they have no idea the device comes from a historian born in Exeter, England, in 1824.

Spalding became a power in the National League, coming up with a reserve system that tied the five best players to every club and imposing a maximum salary of $2,000 per player nearly a century before American sports installed a salary cap. Under Spalding, the owners tightened their control to keep the next generation of players from exerting the free agency he had used to move from Boston to Chicago. Echoing Spalding, Chadwick praised the reserve rule, asserting that "the exorbitant demands" of players would "eventually bankrupt the strongest company in the professional arena."

Having tightened management's grip on the labor pool in his own country, Spalding set out to peddle baseball elsewhere. Hearing about the 1888 centennial planned in Australia, he organized a barnstorming expedition that would take the American game around the world. Twenty major league players signed up for the trip, along with a cricket coach, a manager, two assistants, several journalists, Spalding's mother, and a few other women, along with a balloonist and parachutist named Professor Bartholomew. With Spalding's very active cooperation, there were no black players, yet the great man was not against hiring a black mascot, Clarence Duval from Chicago, who wore the White Stockings' uniform for good luck and was paraded around in front of Asians, Australians, Africans, and Europeans with a leash around his neck, a wonderful advertisement for the American character, indeed.

After a sendoff from President Grover Cleveland at the White House, the entourage left Chicago on October 20, 1888, and traveled west to California. The players practiced cricket on an improvised pitch on board the ship, and played both sports in New Zealand and Australia, without gaining too many converts. Professor Bartholomew was the main attraction, drawing people onto the grounds, but he injured both legs in a hard landing in Ballarat and was put out of commission. The troop continued on to Colombo, Ceylon, having their photographs taken playing ball in the desert sand and sprawling over the Sphinx, in Egypt, and then moved on to Naples, Paris, London, Bristol, Birmingham, Glasgow, Manchester, Liverpool, Belfast, and Dublin.

Upon landing in New York in April of 1889, the entourage was honored at a nine-course banquet (one for every inning) at Delmonico's, attended by Theodore Roosevelt, the future president, and Mark Twain, by then an American celebrity. Twain set an early standard for bombast by calling baseball "the very symbol, the outward and visible expression of the drive, and push, and rush and struggle of the raging, tearing, booming nineteenth century!"

The menu, not unusual for an age that had not discovered calories or self-restraint, included oysters, Ceylon cream of asparagus soup, red snapper, fillet of beef, braised capons, Roman punch, plovers, pudding, fruits, coffee, and cheese. There were also nine toasts, which surely softened up the American burghers for the sales pitch by Abraham G. Mills, a former president of the National League: baseball was "a purely American invention." Upon these words, the players and the guests began pounding on the tables, chanting, "No rounders! No rounders! No rounders!" The trip had formalized Spalding's role as Saint Goodwill the Evangelist. He was taking on not just cricket but all other alien forms of bat-and-ball games. From here on, baseball was to be treated as the American game.

Along with prosperity and expansion came corruption. In 1877, a gambling scandal broke in Louisville, causing four guilty players to be banned, effectively ruining that franchise. Other teams came and went—Providence, Indianapolis, Hartford, Milwaukee—but the industry continued to grow. With players increasingly tied to their team, the owners were able to consolidate the rules, build bigger stadiums, and attract more paying customers through set schedules of games every Tuesday, Thursday, and Saturday.

Modern fans tend to think postseason baseball began with the first World Series in 1903 but from 1882 to 1890, the National League and the American Association met for postseason play eight times, a huge step for public exposure and income. In 1885 and 1886, Chris Von der Ahe's St. Louis Browns met Spalding's White Stockings in a series labeled "the world's championship"—at least that part of the world including adjacent Illinois and Missouri.

The experimentation continued with balls ranging from spongy to rock-hard, often difficult to grip. The pitching was morphing from underhand to overhand. Bats were homemade, ranging from broom-handle thin to fence-post thick. Most infielders stood erect, more or less glued to the base to which they were assigned, at least until pioneers began discovering how much territory they could cover. Charles Comiskey, a handsome player from Chicago, was given credit as one of the early first basemen to play wide of the base, thereby increasing his defensive range. William Arthur (Candy) Cummings, a pitcher who won 124 games for four different teams in the old National Association of Professional Base Ball Players from 1872 through 1875, claimed to have invented the curveball after skipping clamshells on the water. Cummings and the curveball have since provided a cottage industry for scientists intent on proving that a curveball either does or does not exist. (Generations of failed hitters, trudging homeward with their bats and their release papers, would venture the firm scientific conclusion that the ball does, indeed, curve.)

Other great players and characters emerged near the end of the nineteenth century, some of them dying young, often from drink or disease: Charles (Hoss) Radbourne, a right-hander who won 60 games in 1884, still the record for most victories in a season, but died at forty-four; Mike (King) Kelly, whose dashing ways on the base paths inspired the baseball chant "Slide, Kelly, slide," received the first five-figure salary (exactly $10,000), but died at thirty-six; Ed Delahanty, a prolific batter and the oldest of five brothers who reached the major leagues, was thirty-five when he walked off the team's stalled train and fell off the bridge at Niagara Falls, Ontario; Wee Willie Keeler, a five-foot, four-and-a-half-inch, 140-pound outfielder who dexterously slapped the ball into unoccupied corners and said his mission was to "hit 'em where they ain't"; and Billy Sunday, who stole 246 bases in five seasons but then became a prominent evangelist and gave up the game at twenty-seven.

Roger Connor remains the nineteenth-century star who was almost totally forgotten—a slugger from an age when home runs were considered oafish, wasteful, the ruin of a perfectly good rally. Six feet, three inches tall and weighing 220 pounds, the child of Irish immigrants, Connor was summoned down the Hudson River, soon joined by new teammates Buck Ewing and John Montgomery Ward, giving New York three future Hall of Famers at the top of its lineup. In 1885, the team brought in a new manager, Jim Mutrie, who referred to his stars as "my giants," which soon led to the official nickname of that historic franchise.

A deft first baseman who stole 244 bases and hit 233 triples, Connor smashed one home run completely out of the old Polo Grounds in New York, upon which the wealthy box-seat patrons took up a collection and bought Connor a gold watch said to be worth $500. When Connor retired, nobody fussed over his total of 138 homers, clearly the most anybody had ever hit. He went back to Waterbury and bought the local minor league team, and later worked in the school system.

"The family old-timers said he was just a regular family man after his playing days who often helped friends and family out of financial hardships," a grand-nephew, Garrett Squires, recollected early in the twenty-first century. "So he had a good life from all accounts."

Perhaps it was a good life but it was also uncelebrated. In 1921, when Babe Ruth was swatting home runs for the Yankees in the second version of the Polo Grounds, Roger Connor was living a couple of hours away in northern Connecticut. When the Babe hit his 138th home run and then his 139th, Connor was not invited to sit in a box seat of honor to graciously applaud the Babe, as is the custom today when records are broken. He was not mentioned at all. When Connor died in 1931, the obituary in the Waterbury paper played up his contribution to local baseball after he had left the major leagues but it did not note that Connor had once held the record for home runs before Babe Ruth. In 1976, a Waterbury sportswriter hectored the Veterans Committee to vote Roger Connor into the Baseball Hall of Fame. The plaque says Connor was the home run king of the nineteenth century.

The lack of attention paid to Connor was due to the low status of the home run rather than any obscurity of baseball itself. Although generally perceived as rough-hewn characters who would disrupt a hotel or restaurant with their rowdy arrival, many players in the last quadrant of the nineteenth century were celebrities, the subjects of songs, articles, and gossip. Having shed their amateur status, baseball players were regarded in the same class as laborers or tradesmen or music hall performers, with none of the college-boy aura that would later become attached to football or the country-club glamour associated with tennis and golf. In fact, a small percentage of baseball players were college men, like Ward, a lawyer out of Columbia University in New York.

The patronizing air from the stockbrokers and businessmen who bought box seats to the games is detected in the *New York Times*'s coverage of the Delmonico's dinner in April of 1889. Cap Anson, the manager of the White Stockings, who had spent a year at Notre Dame University, was described as appearing "considerably embarrassed when he rose to his feet, but was also thankful that he had been permitted to assist in teaching the world what it most needed to know." In the eyes of the nameless reporter, Anson came off as a humble oaf, which may or may not have had any connection to his staunch opposition to blacks' participating in the major leagues. The *Times* then described how Ward "seemed glad of the opportunity given him to display his singularly correct knowledge of the English language," with the reporter using the better vocabulary of this college man to contrast with the vast majority of the players. Baseball players are still regarded by the public as day laborers, generally of modest class and pedigree, partially because of the rising number of Hispanics in the game, coupled with resentment of high salaries and the strength of the union. When the players do not report for work, they are perceived as committing an injustice to the population, like gardeners and nannies not reporting for work. How can they do this to us?

The polysyllabic Ward became an organizer of the Players' Brotherhood, which led to the rebel Players League in 1890, in reaction to the $2,000 maximum salary and the reserve clause the owners were trying to force on the top players. Among his colleagues in the early Brotherhood were Comiskey, who was managing an upstart team in his hometown of Chicago, and Connie Mack, a lanky catcher from Massachusetts.

"The purpose of our Brotherhood was to protect the players," Mack would say many years later, by which time he and Comiskey were widely depicted as penurious owners in Philadelphia and Chicago, respectively. Comiskey is identified by the 1919 gambling scandal among his resentful players while Mack is identified for twice dismantling his pennant-winning Athletics teams in order to raise cash, yet both started as union men and rebels. Spalding went after the Brotherhood with the help of his dutiful scribe, Chadwick, who claimed the Players League had financial backing from devious Wall Street sources, always a popular, if anonymous, scapegoat. The Players League folded after one year.

Of course, brotherhood went only so far. Blacks who had been freed from slavery and others who had fought for the Union in the Civil War soon excelled at the game. In 1867, an all-black team, the Philadelphia Excelsiors, beat the Brooklyn Uniques, 42–25. That same year, the National Association of Base Ball Players refused to accept black teams. In 1869, the Philadelphia Pythians, also black, completed their second undefeated season. In 1871, Octavius Catto, the manager of the Pythians, was killed in a race riot.

Some blacks had the courage to persist. John W. (Bud) Fowler joined a white professional team in New Castle, Pennsylvania, in 1872, but so many opponents slid into him with their rudimentary spikes that he had to protect himself by taping wooden slats on his legs, perhaps the first recorded use of shin guards. Ultimately, Fowler settled on an all-black touring team named the Page Fence Giants, based in Adrian, Michigan, and barnstorming around the eastern third of the country in their own private railroad car, sometimes playing (and beating) squads of major-leaguers.

Moses Fleetwood Walker, the son of an Ohio doctor and a graduate of Oberlin College and law student, became the first known black major-leaguer in 1884, when he joined the Toledo team of the American Association, followed by his brother, Welday. Some of his teammates accepted Walker, but opposition came from Cap Anson, the star and manager of the Chicago White Stockings, run by none other than Albert Goodwill Spalding. Anson's views were well known. A team in Newark, New Jersey, once fielded a black Canadian pitcher named George Stovey, until Anson shouted, "Get that nigger off the field!" In 1884, after Anson refused to let his team play against the Walkers, the Toledo team began receiving threatening letters, and dropped both men. Walker played for other teams, but he ultimately left the game and led a stormy life that included an acquittal for murder after he had stabbed a man in self-defense. Although more than fifty blacks had played in this period, official baseball was soon completely white.

Spalding, who claimed baseball "elevates and ... fits the American character," sat back while the Walkers were run out of the business. There would not be another recognized African-American player in the so-called major leagues until 1947. By that time, both Spalding and Anson would be enshrined in the Baseball Hall of Fame, a totally bogus setting that Spalding would help to invent.

IV

COLUMBUS, POCAHONTAS, AND DOUBLEDAY

For the past century, Abner Doubleday has been generally accepted as the father of baseball, but only now does the sport officially acknowledge that Doubleday is a twentieth-century invention, a red herring, the man who wasn't there. Doubleday existed, there is no doubt about that. He was a West Point graduate who went on to become a Civil War general with considerable public visibility, but he is also a classic example of the American need to construct our own mythology.

Doubleday never claimed to have invented baseball. Others gave him credit for this, long after he was gone and he suited their purpose. In the late nineteenth century, Americans were still trying to distance themselves from their European origins, having fled across the ocean, seeking religious and political freedom or just enough to eat. There was still enough insecurity over domination by London and Paris that Americans felt the need for their own heroes, their own pioneers, their own artists and writers, their own traditions.

Doubleday is hardly the first or last example of the national need to fib: Was Columbus really the first European to explore North America? Did George Washington really chop down a cherry tree and admit his guilt? Mythmaking always needs new material, including the supposed capture of a soldier, Jessica Lynch, in Iraq or the death of the football player–soldier Pat Tillman in Afghanistan.

The creation of Doubleday as legendary father of the game stemmed from the ideological dispute between Albert Goodwill Spalding and Henry Chadwick. Historians do not know whether Spalding consciously invented Doubleday's role, or whether he slipped into the belief through wishful thinking. In the end, the result was the same.

The scientist and baseball expert Stephen Jay Gould called the Doubleday legend "baseball's creation myth," referring to one side's discovery of scientific evidence of primates straightening up and performing increasingly sophisticated tasks of body and mind over the millennia and the other side's finding that such evidence does not fit their creed.

The collision between Spalding's and Chadwick's visions became apparent at the turn of the century. Spalding wrote a letter to Tim Murnane, a former player who had become a sportswriter in Boston: "Our good old American game of base ball must have an American Dad." In 1903, Chadwick, as the editor of the *Spalding Guide*, wrote that baseball had directly descended from the old British game of rounders. Having been born in England, Chadwick eagerly accepted baseball as the quintessential American pastime but was merely pointing out its complicated roots leading back to England.

Spalding, like many turn-of-the-century Americans, was vigorously aware of the growing power and size of the young country. Two years later, the *Spalding Guide* carried bravado from A.G. himself: "I hereby challenge the Grand Old Man of Base Ball to produce his proofs and demonstrate in some tangible way, if he can, that our national game derived its origin from Rounders." Of course there was proof, although it was not as easily attainable as it would become a century later, when the most rudimentary search of the Internet can come up with copious legitimate lists of ancient bat-and-ball references.

Spalding seemed to need the big-bang theory of baseball to justify his patriotism. In 1906 he appointed Abraham G. Mills, the former president of the National League and a vice president of the Otis Elevator Co., to lead a national board to investigate baseball's roots. This was the very same Mills who had hammered home the American origins of baseball during that nine-course banquet at Delmonico's in 1889, leading to grown men pounding on the table and chanting: "No rounders! No rounders! No rounders!" Mills was now back for a second tour of duty in the table-pounding department.

The seven members of the Mills committee were all reputable but none was a scholar or a researcher, nor did they have a staff to perform even basic tasks of culling information. As unheard of as this may be in contemporary America, their sole job seemed to be justifying a set belief.

In 1907, Spalding came up with two letters from Abner Graves, a mining engineer in Colorado, who was originally from the village of Cooperstown in upstate New York. Graves recalled Abner Doubleday stopping a marbles game in front of a tailor shop to teach baseball to the youths of Cooperstown—"Abner Doubleday being then a boy pupil of 'Green's Select School,'" Graves added. At times, Graves was vague about the exact year of Doubleday's "invention," but ultimately he settled on 1839, when he would have been five and Doubleday would have been twenty.

Doubleday was born on June 26, 1819, in Ballston Spa, approximately seventy-five miles from Cooperstown, and grew up in Auburn, far west of that area. His father, Ulysses, had been baptized in Cooperstown, but there is no specific evidence of Abner's ever setting foot in the town. He entered West Point on September 1, 1838, and in 1839 he would surely have been court-martialed had he been discovered nearly 100 miles away from the academy, playing a ball game. There is no record of him leaving the academy during that time, nor is there any trace of his involvement with baseball.

"You ask for some information as to how I passed my youth," Doubleday once responded to a letter from a citizen, late in his military career. "I was brought up in a book store and early imbibed a taste for reading. I was fond of poetry and much interested in mathematical studies. In my outdoor sports, I was addicted to topographical work and even as a boy amused myself by making maps of the country around my father's residence, which was in Auburn, N.Y."

Doubleday was commissioned from the Military Academy in 1842 and served in Monterrey, Mexico. On April 12, 1861, he fired the first shot at rebel troops menacing Fort Sumter, and later he served at Bull Run and Antietam with a minor role at Gettysburg, helping to repel Pickett's fatal charge.

Baseball had grown popular among both the blue and gray soldiers of the time, but in Doubleday's entire life there is only one single link with the sport: in 1871, when he was finishing his career in charge of an all-black regiment at Fort McKavett, Texas, he requested baseball equipment for his troops, for recreation.

Doubleday retired from the military in 1873 and used his scientific skills to help build the first cable car railway in San Francisco. He died at the age of seventy-four on January 26, 1893, in Mendham, New Jersey, and was buried in Arlington National Cemetery. A decade after his death, Doubleday was advanced as the father of a game he apparently had never played or discussed.

Ulysses Doubleday's older brother, Demas, did live in Springfield, just to the north of Cooperstown, and in 1829 he had a son, Abner Demas Doubleday, who lived around Cooperstown until after the Civil War. In his addled later years, Graves could have confused Abner Demas Doubleday with the future general, despite the ten-year gap in their ages.

Mills's connection is complicated, in that he had been a friend of Doubleday and had served in the honor guard when Doubleday's body lay in state in New York's City Hall. The findings by the Mills commission were published in Spalding's next baseball guide in March of 1908, but were signed by only one person—Mills himself. The league presidents verified the findings but Chadwick died that spring without responding to the official linking of Doubleday and baseball.

In June of 1924, Graves, then ninety, shot and killed his second wife, Minnie, in a dispute over the sale of their house. He died in a state asylum for the criminally insane in Pueblo, Colorado, in the fall of 1926. His troubled old age would seem to cast doubts on his flickering memories of a childhood experience in Cooperstown—but he was Spalding's star witness, his only witness, and he served a purpose. With its relatively short history, the United States was quite well served by the prospect that a prominent general had dreamed up the game in one of the thirteen original states, that the sport was a purely American invention.

Spalding's mischief went a long way. In 1935, a distant relative of Abner Graves found a scruffy and tattered baseball in a farmhouse in Fly Creek, just outside Cooperstown. The so-called Fly Creek

Ball somehow wound up being accepted as the talisman and proof of Doubleday's involvement with the game. The absolute lack of proof would not reach critical mass for many decades. In the meantime, lucky old baseball was about to gain a core, a home, a central place where everybody could celebrate the American game. The Hall would become the most popular sports museum in the country, and Albert Spalding would remain a hallowed figure, despite his strange involvement in the Doubleday myth.

The old pitcher became a wealthy man through his sporting goods empire, which included *Spalding's Official Baseball Guide,* first published in 1876, plus the manufacture of uniforms, bats, balls, croquet equipment, ice skates, fishing gear, tennis racquets, dumbbells, shoes, caps, hunting goods, and bicycles.

The Spalding name survives in the memory of generations of city children who played ball games (punchball, stickball, stoopball) with the lively pink ball manufactured by the Spalding company. Lifetime reputations were made by neighborhood heroes who could hit a pink ball the distance of three sewer manholes, or punch a pink ball off the brick wall of a grade school. In New York, when I grew up, any bouncy pink ball was called a spaldeen.

———

Like generations of Americans, old A.G. left Chicago and moved to a warmer clime—Point Loma, California, where he ran for the Senate, and lost. His wife, Josie, died in 1899 but he soon married Elizabeth Mayer Churchill, with whom he already had a son, who was promptly renamed Albert Goodwill Spalding, Jr.

This second marriage, with its background of scandal, raises a connection between Spalding and Doubleday: the second Mrs. Spalding had become interested in Theosophy, a spiritual movement, and the old pitcher became president of the American Theosophical Society. In his later years, Doubleday had subscribed to the Transcendentalist journal the *Dial* and had attended spiritual gatherings in the White House with President and Mrs. Lincoln. At the very least, Spalding, in California, would have been aware of Doubleday through their mutual interest in Theosophy. Aside from Graves's two letters, it is unclear why Spalding settled on

Doubleday as the father of baseball. Was it a cynical act or wishful thinking? We may never know. Spalding died on September 9, 1915, at the age of sixty-five, his funeral held at the Theosophy center, known as the Temple of Aryans.

———

The sport lucked out with the setting of the Hall, in a charming corner of Americana. The burghers of Cooperstown disregarded any questions about the Doubleday myth, and opened the Hall in time for the alleged centennial year of 1939. Members of the Baseball Writers Association of America voted in 1936 for the first entering class, with Ty Cobb, Babe Ruth, Honus Wagner, Walter Johnson, and Christy Mathewson all receiving the necessary 75 percent. The next year, Tris Speaker was chosen, along with Napoleon Lajoie and Cy Young. In 1938, Grover Cleveland Alexander was chosen, and in 1939, George Sisler, Eddie Collins, and Wee Willie Keeler were picked, among others. The same year, Lou Gehrig, whose fatal illness had just been diagnosed, was quickly installed, as the Hall bypassed its rule that a player must have been retired for five years. Chadwick was chosen in 1938 as a builder of the game and Spalding followed in 1939.

The first induction ceremony was held on June 12, 1939, with many of the honorees in attendance, but not all. Back home, working as a greeter in a bar, Alexander was quoted as saying: "The Hall of Fame is fine, but it doesn't mean bread and butter. It's only your picture on the wall."

Alexander's pragmatism was soon overwhelmed by the newfound passion for the Hall. Old players lived out their lives hoping to be tapped for the Hall, however belatedly. In reality, there are about five levels of the Hall of Fame, ranging from giants like Babe Ruth to friends of friends or beneficiaries of myth and sentimentality. Fans, writers, and baseball people spend years advocating oldtimers who have been slighted by the selection process, first by the baseball writers or later by a panel of old-timers. For many years, Ted Williams was a huge political force on the review committee, paving the way for players he admired—most notably, his old teammate Bobby Doerr and his old rival Phil Rizzuto.

Williams became a voice of conscience, perhaps because of his own childhood experiences with intolerance, since his mother was a Mexican-American in San Diego. During his induction speech in 1966, Williams made an emphatic request: "I hope that some day Satchel Paige and Josh Gibson will be voted into the Hall of Fame as symbols of the great Negro players who are not here only because they weren't given the chance." People listened to the justice in Williams's thundering tones: in 1971, Paige was voted into the Hall, since followed by seventeen other Negro Leagues players— all in the main wing, as total equals. Early in 2006, the Hall held a mass election and accepted seventeen other prominent veterans of the Negro Leagues.

For every player voted into the Hall, however belatedly, there are others who fall short of the mysterious shifting line. Hearts are broken every year when beloved hitters like Tony Oliva and Gil Hodges or durable pitchers like Tommy John and Jim Kaat are once again passed over.

———

For a long time, the Hall went along with the Doubleday legend but in the past generation it has become a repository not only for artifacts but for verifiable history. The Graves letters, lost but recovered in 1997, are no more enlightening than they were in Mills's time. Years ago somebody took down the sign "Birthplace of Baseball" from the Cooperstown exit off the New York State Thruway. There is still a Doubleday Field in Cooperstown, where every year two major league teams play an exhibition, in homage to the man who apparently never played the game in his life.

The Hall keeps growing into a sophisticated, multimedia, online, year-round haven of souvenirs and records, available to serious researchers or casual tourists mainly interested in souvenir T-shirts of their favorite member of the Hall. Yet the Hall is saved from being totally Disneyfied by its location in sleepy upstate New York. The sport also got lucky because the annual induction takes place at the end of July, when little else is happening. No other sport is blessed with the living Norman Rockwell tableau of the induction ceremony: fans pile into rooming houses and bed-and-breakfasts around Cooperstown and chase down autographs from the stars; agile boys hang from tree branches and gape as the old players weep while being inducted into the Hall.

In the evening, aging members of the Hall sit on wicker chairs in view of the classic American lake, Otsego, straight out of James Fenimore Cooper, and they tell stories about the old days. Baseball is all about stories, many of which are even true.

V

GROWING PAINS

The newly established league had one gaping hole: it did not have a team in New York. And that would not do. Ban Johnson, the president, was a Midwesterner, but he knew that any outfit that dared to call itself the American League needed a franchise in the big city.

A large man with large ambitions, Johnson had been a sportswriter in Cincinnati before he became president of the Western League in 1893. He found investors and players for his league, cracking down on gambling and crude behavior, and in 1901, Johnson changed the name to the American League, going against the westward flow of population to establish himself on the eastern seaboard.

The twentieth century could now officially begin. Charles Comiskey's franchise was moved from St. Paul, Minnesota, to Chicago, and in 1902 the Milwaukee Brewers became the St. Louis Browns. Under Johnson's aggressive recruiting of players, his league outdrew the National League, prompting an agreement that made the leagues equals and competitors in 1903.

Then came the move that would change the American League forever: Johnson encouraged the Baltimore team to transfer to New York, only a mile or two from the haughty Giants of the National League. Located on a plateau in upper Manhattan, the High-landers, or Hilltoppers, would wallow in mediocrity or worse for nearly two decades, by which time the team had changed its name again. The new nickname was Yankees.

After that flurry of musical chairs in the early years of the century, the two major leagues coalesced into a stable enterprise of eight teams apiece, starting in 1903. The American League consisted of the Highlanders, St. Louis Browns, Chicago White Stockings, Boston Puritans or Pilgrims, Detroit Tigers, Cleveland Indians, Philadelphia Athletics, and Washington Nationals, while the National teams were the Boston Braves, Brooklyn Superbas, New York Giants, Philadelphia Phillies, Pittsburgh Pirates, Cincinnati

Reds, Chicago Cubs, and St. Louis Cardinals. These sixteen franchises would remain in place for a solid half century. How many institutions can say that?

Every sport needs its rivalries. The first feud of the century was between Johnson and pugnacious John J. McGraw, who had moved from Baltimore to the Giants in 1902. A former infielder from St. Bonaventure University in upstate New York, McGraw advocated the scrappy style the Orioles had played a decade earlier, with wiry and hungry athletes slashing line drives for doubles and triples, tossing their elbows and sharpening their spikes. In the eyes of Muggsy McGraw, the home run was essentially a novelty item.

McGraw soon took on the entire upstart American League, calling the financially challenged Athletics "white elephants." Connie Mack, their owner-manager, proudly adopted a white elephant as his team's symbol. Willowy at six feet, one inch tall and 150 pounds, the former catcher struck a more dignified pose than McGraw. Born Cornelius McGillicuddy in East Brookfield, Massachusetts, he shortened his name to please the fans or perhaps the newspaper typesetters.

When he was long past wearing a uniform, Mack wore a conservative suit in his dugout, just like the bankers who filed into the ballpark at closing hour. Year in, year out, he would strike his characteristic pose, rolling up a scorecard in one hand and giving signals to the men in uniform. As a former player, with no outside income, Mack did not have the luxury of considering himself a sportsman but instead was at the mercy of the attendance and his team's position in the standings. He was strapped by Philadelphia's position as the last major league city to have blue laws, which until 1934 forbade baseball games and other entertainment on Sunday. This restriction meant the Athletics often had to travel overnight to play Sunday games elsewhere. Mack would be vilified for selling off his best players, but that tactic would be used by many other cash-strapped owners over the years.

Despite McGraw's yapping at the American League, the owners agreed on the moneymaking potential of a postseason championship series, the first since 1890. The Pittsburgh team from the

National League played Boston of the American League in a best-of-nine format in 1903, starting with three games at Boston, followed by four in Pittsburgh and then returning to Boston for what turned out to be Boston's clinching in the eighth game. The Boston management was unprepared for huge crowds but was not about to turn away paying customers, even though the crowd threatened to spill onto the field. A group of fans called the Royal Rooters, led by Nuf Ced McGreevey, incessantly sang a show tune, "Tessie," and many people felt the energy unleashed by the song had powered Boston to victory.

The term "World Series" has an ironic ring these days, given the high level of play in some Asian and Latin American countries, but in those days the name pretty much reflected the only powerhouse in the world. As grandiose as it was, the name "World Series" fit the optimistic mood of the fast-growing republic. McGraw ratcheted up his feud with Johnson and refused to let his Giants play the defending champions from Boston in 1904, but the following season McGraw was persuaded to behave and the Giants won the resumption of the World Series.

The new century had its stars, known all over the country: Ty Cobb, the Georgia Peach; deceptively stocky Honus Wagner; the durable pitcher Cy Young, who would win 192 games for Boston in the first eight years of the American League. The most popular player of all was Christy Mathewson, out of Bucknell College in rural Pennsylvania, who kept his promise to his mother that he would not pitch on the Sabbath and soon became the first national example of the gentleman athlete, contradicting baseball's rowdy image.

Known as Big Six—either for his height of six feet, one and a half inches, or a popular fire engine or early automobile—Mathewson threw a pitch he called the fadeaway, which broke the opposite way from the normal right-handed orbit. He pitched virtually every third game, ultimately winning 373 and losing 188.

The composed Mathewson and the tempestuous McGraw became close friends, the original odd couple, sharing a Manhattan apartment along with their wives. Although Mathewson could be distant, the public respected him for his pitching, his high standards, and his handsome features. Then he became baseball's foremost casualty of war.

When the Great War broke out in Europe in 1914, the United States tried to ignore it, and did not enter the conflict until April of 1917. With war dragging on, America faced a challenge to its isolationist posture. When anonymous young Americans began to die in the forests and fields of Europe, the American sport faced pressure to respond. In May of 1918, the United States adopted a "work-or-fight" policy for able-bodied men, the first time any American sport had been under public pressure to respond to a national crisis. Since baseball had postured itself as the embodiment of national values, its players were under pressure to either join a defense industry or volunteer for the military. For most of them, the war would be a brief inconvenience, but Eddie Grant, the Harvard graduate and captain of the Giants, became the only major-leaguer to die directly from combat, when he was killed in the Argonne Forest while fighting to rescue the Lost Battalion.

In August of 1918, at the age of thirty-eight, Mathewson signed up for the war out of a sense of responsibility. By now he was the manager of the Cincinnati Reds because his close friend, McGraw, had made sure he had a job when his arm wore out. Mathewson joined the Chemical Warfare Services, along with two other future members of the Hall of Fame—Tyrus Raymond Cobb, thirty-two, the eleven-time batting champion, and Branch Wesley Rickey, thirty-eight, the cerebral college man, once a marginal catcher but now the president of the Browns.

These three relatively elderly soldiers were sent to France, near the Belgian border. Mathewson arrived with the flu, which would soon kill millions of people around the world, and then, in a training exercise, Mathewson accidentally inhaled murderous mustard gas. Later he took another dose of gas near the front. After the Armistice on November 11, 1918, Mathewson returned home a weakened and aged man and he later caught tuberculosis, dying at forty-five.

Cobb was the antithesis of Matty and Rickey, two college men and respecters of the Sabbath. An umpire-baiter, spike-sharpener, fan-fighter, and teammate-battler with racist tendencies, Cobb became the first great hitter of the century, batting .366 over 24 seasons. Unpopular with opponents and teammates alike, Cobb confirmed the image of baseball players as crude and uneducated and sometimes even racist.

At the same time, many players were lionized, often appearing in vaudeville music halls in the off-season, recognized through their photographs in magazines and the copious newspapers of the time. Some were immortalized by doggerel like "Baseball's Sad Lexicon," by Franklin Pierce Adams in New York's *Evening Mail* of July 10, 1910, lauding the Cubs' double-play combination of shortstop Joe Tinker, second baseman Johnny Evers, and first baseman Frank Chance.

> These are the saddest of possible words:
> "Tinker to Evers to Chance."
> Trio of bear cubs, and fleeter than birds,
> Tinker and Evers and Chance.
> Ruthlessly pricking our gonfalon bubble,
> Making a Giant hit into a double—
> Words that are heavy with nothing but trouble:
> "Tinker to Evers to Chance."

Adams's tribute was not as cosmically inventive as the citing of Abner Doubleday as the inventor of baseball, but these eight lines became embedded in the minds of fans everywhere, and perhaps even sportswriters. Tinker, Evers, and Chance were all fine players, who played together as a unit for 10 years, a rarity then and now, but they were not an unprecedented double-play machine, either. In direct response to Adams's little ditty, all three were eventually voted into the Hall of Fame, Evers in 1939 and his teammates in 1946.

While accumulating a folklore, the young industry of baseball was also developing new labor and financial problems. In 1913, the Fraternity of Professional Baseball Players was founded, leading to the outlaw Federal League of 1914, which raided the two major leagues. Connie Mack's A's won four pennants from 1910 through

1914, but after Chief Bender and Eddie Plank jumped to the Federal League, and Home Run Baker sat out a season in a salary dispute, Mack tore apart his team even further, selling a number of players to the Red Sox (who would soon move their better players to the Yankees). The A's soon hit bottom. "The Federal League wrecked my club by completely changing the spirit of my players," Mack would claim.

The two established leagues survived a restraint-of-trade suit by the upstart Federal League. In 1915, a Chicago federal judge, Kenesaw Mountain Landis, said he was "shocked" that anybody could possibly consider baseball to be "labor." It was a game, Landis ruled, and, as a national institution, it was not subject to interstate commerce laws. This decision by Landis was vital to the owners because it strengthened the reserve clause, which appeared to bind players to their clubs for the length of their careers, or until they were traded, sold, or discarded. The reserve clause would dominate the industry for the next six decades.

As the war dragged on, attendance was down in the 1918 World Series, which led to a dispute over the size of World Series shares. Before the fifth game, the Red Sox and Cubs demanded minimum shares of $1,500 and $1,000 for winning and losing, respectively, insisting they were prepared to cancel the game. When baseball officials worried that a strike could cause a riot, the players gave in, starting the game an hour late. In the end, the Red Sox were paid only $1,108 per player and the Cubs $671 each. This strike threat was one of the justifications the Red Sox' ownership would use for dealing Babe Ruth to the Yankees at the end of 1919. Management convinced reporters in Boston and New York to depict Ruth as a malingerer, not just because of his undisciplined habits but also because of his salary demands and his role as potential striker.

With the owners receiving fawning decisions like that of Judge Landis, and with a growing public perception that baseball was the national game, the players were burdened with the expectation that they were somehow above labor grievances. Many players saw themselves as underpaid and exploited. The stage was set for baseball's first major scandal.

VI

THE BLACK SOX

They are the lost boys of baseball, lashed together, eight of them, in a ship that can never return to harbor. Even today, as the eight exiles from the 1919 Chicago White Sox bob outside the boundaries of their sport, they are a living reminder of what can go wrong when leadership fails.

Christy Mathewson could see it happening, right below him. Weakened from his wartime gassing, he had been unable to resume his job as manager of the Reds, but agreed to write about the 1919 World Series for the *New York World.* He sat in the press box next to his friend Hugh Fullerton of the *Chicago Herald and Examiner,* who had been warned of a possible gambling conspiracy.

The former pitcher and the diligent reporter watched the body language and the positioning, not merely the hits and the errors. They spotted the White Sox' catcher, Ray (Cracker) Schalk, arguing with Lefty Williams, one of the Sox' best pitchers, out near the mound, and detected Kid Gleason, the manager, in a visible fury. The two friends operated on the theory that hitters hated to give up base hits and, if they wanted to hurt their own team, would much prefer to botch a play on defense. Mathewson and Fullerton began circling suspicious defensive plays by some of the most adept fielders on the Sox—not overt fumbles or bad throws but perhaps a slight hesitancy or elliptical route to the ball, turning a single into a double, just enough to affect a game.

Few fans picked up on these nuances. The nation had been stunned by the whiff of mortality during the war that had affected even a golden man like Mathewson. Once able to pitch every few days, he was now a pale specter hunched over his scorecard. The prevalent mood of the nation—even with Prohibition on the way—was, *Let's have a drink.*

Certainly, the baseball owners were not looking for trouble. The game had bounced back, attendance leaped from 3 million in 1918 to 6.5 million in 1919. Happy days were here again. The owners had not developed any centralized leadership, making Ban Johnson the most powerful executive, giving him freedom to feud with renegade owners as well as successive National League presidents. The friendly ruling by Judge Landis in Chicago had enforced the owners' control of the players.

Like the rest of the country, the owners wanted a respite from the sudden chilling awareness that America was linked to the rest of the world. People were back at work, making money, investing money, spending money. The game was one other way of forgetting. Gambling was another. The managing job had opened up for Mathewson in Cincinnati because the Reds' ownership had been hesitant to choose the more logical candidate, Hal Chase, the stylish first baseman, who had a reputation as a gambler. McGraw had volunteered his surrogate son, Mathewson, as an alternative to the high-living first baseman known as Prince Hal.

As a novice manager, Mathewson observed Chase occasionally bungle a play by making a slightly inaccurate toss to the pitcher or fail to reach a ground ball, plays he would normally make with ease. Mathewson learned that Chase had handed a young pitcher $50, saying he had bet on the Reds to lose, but the charge was ignored by John Heydler, the weak president of the National League. Mathewson inexplicably shipped Chase to his friend McGraw, who, by 1918, banished Chase from the Giants. The long tolerance of Chase had built up a climate of gambling in baseball. Now there were volunteers for a bigger scandal.

———

In 1919, gamblers found disillusioned players on the South Side of Chicago, toiling for the White Sox of Charles Comiskey. Once an artist at first base and a key member of an early players association, Comiskey now showed nothing but disdain for the current players, who were bound to him by the reserve clause. He had accumulated a superlative squad, but paid most players far below the norm. Eddie Collins, from Columbia University, made sure his $14,500 salary was guaranteed when he came over from Connie Mack's Athletics, but Joe Jackson, the great hitter, illiterate and vulnerable, was paid only $6,000 a year. Many players also felt Comiskey failed to honor bonus agreements, leading to a gnawing sense they were being exploited. In the definitive book on the scandal, *Eight Men Out,* published in 1963, Eliot Asinof blames Comiskey for the players' willingness to be corrupted, and so does John Sayles's brooding movie of the same name, which came out a quarter of a century later.

Late in the 1919 season, as the White Sox prepared to play the Reds in the World Series, various characters buzzed around the Sox, trying to find somebody to corrupt. They found their man in Chick Gandil, a skillful first baseman who had turned thirty-two and was looking to make one big score before his career ran out.

Like many clubs, even the most successful, the White Sox were split into factions based on education, temperament, and region. Seeking teammates who would go along, Gandil studiously avoided Collins, the captain and second baseman, and Schalk, the peppery little catcher.

Gandil ultimately contacted seven other players. Buck Weaver, the third baseman, apparently sat in on the first meeting but never participated or discussed the plot. However, Gandil gained at least tacit approval from Eddie Cicotte and Williams, the two best pitchers, as well as Oscar (Happy) Felsch, the center fielder, Fred McMullin, a reserve infielder, Swede Risberg, the shortstop, and Joe Jackson, the right fielder, one of the great hitters of his time or any other time.

The gamblers, as dysfunctional as the eight White Sox players, could produce only $10,000 before the start of the Series. Gandil invested it all in Cicotte, a veteran pitcher with a family, a mortgage, and a grudge against Comiskey.

As the best-of-nine Series opened in Cincinnati, there was a new player in this crooked game, as dominant in his world as Joe Jackson was in his. Arnold Rothstein from New York was less of a gambler than a believer in sure things. He did not want to confirm his bet until he had a sign that the fix was in, so he told his intermediaries that Cicotte should hit the first batter with a pitch, as a sign of good faith. Keeping track in New York, Rothstein watched the Teletype clatter that Cicotte had hit Morrie Rath with the first pitch, and only then did Rothstein lay down $100,000 on the Reds. Cicotte paid off, lasting only three innings in a 9–1 loss. Other players in on the plot began demanding their share of the money, but Williams came through with one wild inning in a 4–2 loss, putting the White Sox behind, two games to none.

Many fans and bettors, stunned to see the favored White Sox falling behind so decisively, traded rumors of a blatant dump. Comiskey, knowing the high talent level of his players, sensed something was wrong and late one night shared his concerns with Heydler, the president of the rival league. Comiskey would not have this conversation with Johnson, the president of his own league, because the two of them despised each other. Heydler relayed Comiskey's concerns to Johnson, whose reaction was: "That is the whelp of a beaten cur."

Inevitably, the seven active participants became resentful when the next installment of payoffs did not come through. Most of them reverted to trying hard on every play, which made it easier for Dickie Kerr, a small rookie pitcher, to win the third game for Chicago. Cicotte and Williams made sure the White Sox lost the fourth and fifth games at home and the Series reverted to Cincinnati, where Kerr won again. Cicotte, perhaps sensing this plot would all come crashing down on him, pitched his best in the seventh game and won. But when the Series returned to Chicago for the eighth game, Williams was warned by a menacing stranger that his family would be harmed if he did not cooperate. The Reds scored four runs in the first inning, and soon Cincinnati became the champion. Arnold Rothstein made a bundle, mostly by not betting on individual games but by wisely trusting the dumpers to perform their task in the longer run. Other gamblers were not so wise, betting the wrong way in games the White Sox won.

Mathewson, for all the circles on his scorecard and his history with Hal Chase in Cincinnati, never referred to the discrepancies when he filed his newspaper articles from the Series. Fullerton, who had predicted the Sox would win, made not-very-reassuring comments that, despite rumors of a gambling coup, the Reds were winning on the up-and-up. At the same time, Ring Lardner, the author and columnist with the *Chicago Tribune*, made some sour comments in print and even directed pointed remarks at the White Sox players during the Series. He was said to have sung a parody of "I'm Forever Blowing Bubbles" that included the lyrics "I'm forever blowing ball games, and the gamblers treat us fair."

In the media circus of the twenty-first century, one would like to think that an open cabal by eight players on one team would surely come to the attention, or at least the paranoia, of assorted reporters, announcers, and bloggers—but look how long it took for all of us to pay attention to the steroids plague of the late 1990s. At most, the few public hints prodded Comiskey to release a statement that said, in part, "I believe my boys fought the battles of the recent World Series on the level, as they have always done." He did, however, withhold the eight players' World Series shares, $3,154.27 each, and announced a reward of $20,000 for any information about a gambling scandal. In mid-November he released the eight checks to the players, presumably hoping the scandal would blow over. It did not.

By the end of the 1920 season, the scandal was investigated by a grand jury in Chicago. The players were so uneducated that they allowed Comiskey's staff to furnish them free legal advice, which was to cooperate with the grand jury, on the promise the club would protect them. Jackson, who depended on his wife to read his contracts, spoke openly to the grand jury, without benefit of counsel. The players were found not guilty, and celebrated in public, assuming they could play the following season.

The owners, however, realized they needed to restore some semblance of faith in baseball. Some had grown tired of the power Ban Johnson had wielded over the years and on November 12, 1920, they hired a commissioner, the very same Chicago federal judge, Kenesaw Mountain Landis, who had given them such a favorable decision back in the 1915 Federal League case. (Landis had acquired his name because his father, a Union medic, had been shot in the leg during a Civil War battle at Kennesaw Mountain outside Marietta, Georgia. The dropping of one "n" appears to have been nothing more than a misspelling.)

With his thick shock of white hair and his rugged profile backing up his cachet as the owners' new hammer, Landis summarily banned all eight players for life. "Birds of a feather flock together," he said in a press release. "Men associating with gamblers and crooks could expect no leniency."

None of the eight Black Sox would ever play organized ball again. Weaver, in particular, seemed shocked at being banished, since by all accounts he had never cooperated with the plot, or taken money, or slacked off during the Series. He had failed to report what he had heard, and that was quite enough for Landis and the suddenly militant owners. The eight players, who ranged from sinister (Gandil) to naive (Weaver), were linked for life, and beyond. Their expulsion from the Garden would stand as the game's Original Sin, haunting the White Sox franchise into the next century.

While Judge Landis made an example of the eight White Sox, he proved to be more hesitant about lifetime punishment for two great players, Ty Cobb and Tris Speaker, who had apparently fixed a game in 1919 that affected the final standings. When that incident surfaced in 1926, Cobb was managing Detroit and Speaker Cleveland. Landis stepped back while Ban Johnson solved that problem by transferring both stars to other teams in 1927. So much for frontier justice.

The punishment stuck on Shoeless Joe Jackson. Long after his death in 1951, he was adopted by no less an authority than Ted Williams, who spent his final decades urging that Jackson and his .356 career batting average be included in the Hall of Fame. The aging Williams, whose career average was .344, would rouse his most blustery logic in defense of his fellow slugger but to no avail.

To justify its place as the national sport, baseball had come up with new penalties for gambling and fixing games, thus setting a tone for good-of-the-game decisions in future decades. There was some debate whether the public, now fully involved in the festivities of the Roaring Twenties, really cared. The fans were still drawn to the game, not necessarily because of the zealous Judge Landis but because of a lusty slugger named George Herman Ruth.

VII

THE BABE

Baseball has always relied heavily on luck, touching the right nerves, somehow working its way into privileged folk status. Never was it luckier than in the wake of the Black Sox scandal, when Babe Ruth saved baseball—and saves it still, truth be told. With Barry Bonds and other latter-day sluggers permanently tainted by steroid suspicions, the good old Babe looks better and better.

Ruth was not only the greatest player in the history of the game but he was also a rollicking, likable, outsized character who arrived at precisely the right moment. He dominated the nation during a decade devoted to change (women gained the vote in 1920) and avoidance (Prohibition was enacted that very same year, and promptly bypassed by a huge swath of the country). Who better to personify this coming-of-age decade, the Roaring Twenties, than a barrel-chested, pigeon-toed hedonist known as the Babe?

America was full of individualists, the descendants of wanderers who had escaped the castes and laws of Europe to seek one freedom or another in the New World. The result was a continent full of people who did not necessarily accept what officials and teachers and pastors told them. George Herman Ruth certainly lived up to that tradition of independence from societal niceties. In a land of open space and mighty rivers and looming mountain ranges, Ruth, too, was a force of nature, a latter-day Paul Bunyan. Coming from Baltimore, where Wee Willie Keeler had "hit 'em where they ain't," Ruth developed his own version of that philosophy—in this case, over fences. He refined the home run as America's definitive sporting act—emphatic, sudden, powerful. Fans plunked down their quarters and their dollars to watch this extrovert perform the extroverted act of slugging a home run.

Nine decades after Ruth's transition into slugger, America is still fascinated by the home run. On television, young and noisy male broadcasters—you could generically label them the Silly Boys—

whoop with amazement at video clips of thick-necked sluggers propelling the ball far into the night.

To this day, I still love talking about, reading about, writing about the Babe. He transcends the decades, the styles, the changes, the races, the money. He is America's beloved prodigal bad-boy son. He *is* baseball.

Before dispatching all these home runs, Ruth was a left-handed pitcher, one of the best in the game. To fully appreciate Babe Ruth, one has to start with his pitching record: 94 victories, 46 losses, and a 2.28 earned run average. If you did not know better, you would glance at his truncated pitching career in some baseball almanac and you would ask: Who *was* that guy? Why did he stop pitching? Did he leave the game? Did he hurt his arm? Did he get in trouble? Imagine what he could have become if he had stayed on the mound.

Ruth came along in 1914, a big lefty just turned nineteen, with virtually no discipline, which was understandable given his Dickensian childhood. He was born in the brawling dock and railroad area of downtown Baltimore to parents too busy serving beer to gandy dancers and stevedores to pay attention to their unruly son. When he was eight, Ruth was placed in the St. Mary's Industrial School for Boys, where he was visited irregularly by his mother, Kate, and sister, Mamie, but never by his father. At the home, the young man was befriended by Brother Matthias Boutier, who recognized his athletic skill and his desire, and channeled him past the tailoring lessons and classroom lectures the kid hated.

When the baseball scouts began finding their way behind the walls of the home, Brother Matthias arranged for Jack Dunn, the owner of the Orioles, to become Ruth's legal guardian. When Dunn signed Ruth for $600 and sent him off to his first spring training in 1914, one of the Orioles' coaches said, "There's one of Jack Dunn's babes." The name stuck. Baseball had better nicknames, back then.

The minor league Orioles quickly sold Ruth to the Red Sox, who used him in four games in 1914. The next three years, still raw, Ruth won 65 games and lost 33, not letting a hasty marriage in Boston slow down his major league carousing. At first he was a novelty as a slugging pitcher, striking nine homers in his first three seasons, but by 1918 he was too valuable to be left on the bench three days out of four. The Sox played him in the outfield or at first base, producing 11 homers and a .300 batting average. In the 1918 World Series he won both his starts with a 1.06 earned run average. By then it was clear: there had never been a player like Babe Ruth. In 1919 he pitched only 17 times in his 130 games, hitting 29 home runs to break the major league home run record.

Given his obvious power, Ruth could very well have saved baseball as a member of the Sox for the next decade or two, but he was destined to save a different franchise in another city. His absence would haunt Boston's fans for eighty-six years, many of them miserable.

Ruth's departure began with the owner of the Red Sox, Harry Frazee, a theatrical impresario and real estate owner from New York, who had no ties to Boston. Caught in a feud with Ban Johnson and most of the American League power structure, Frazee began dealing with the only team that would work with him. The Yankees had never won anything since escaping Baltimore in 1903 but had been bought in 1915 by two rich and ambitious New Yorkers, Jacob Ruppert, a brewing magnate, and Tillinghast l'Hommedieu Huston, an engineer.

In the fall of 1919, as the gambling scandal in Chicago was going public, Ruth was assailed in the Boston press for making exorbitant salary demands on the club. He had signed for $10,000 a year for three seasons, starting in 1919, but after hitting 29 homers that year he demanded $20,000 the next year. Frazee's solution was to sell him to the Yankees, officially announced in January of 1920, for $125,000 plus the promise of a $350,000 loan for Frazee.

Some Boston fans were mortified and others said good riddance, but certainly no one could have predicted this big lummox would become the great transforming figure of the sport. Nobody knew he would become, as it were, Babe Ruth. At twenty-five, Ruth pitched only once for the Yankees in 1920, hitting 54 home runs, nearly doubling his own record.

Legend has it that Judge Landis, in reaction to the Black Sox, ordered up livelier balls so the Babe could drill them over the fences.

As with many other legends, the truth may be more complicated. There is evidence that sporting goods companies had begun, as early as 1910, to use better technology and uniform production techniques to wrap baseballs more tightly around more uniform cork centers and a higher grade of wool, thereby making the balls bounce harder and farther. Years later, the A. J. Reach Company confirmed that in 1919 it had been using new machines and a better grade of Australian wool yarn, which could have caused more tightly wrapped balls to fly farther off the bat, but some of this may have been normal evolution in manufacturing. For whatever reason, the number of home runs jumped from 448 to 630 from 1919 to 1920, but the concept of baseball's new and intentional weapons of mass destruction may have been exaggerated.

Ruth's record-breaking 59 home runs helped the Yankees win their first pennant in 1921 but they would lose the World Series to their landlords, the Giants. The rivalry and larger crowds in the Polo Grounds might have satisfied some baseball people but John J. McGraw was not fond of either the home run or Ruth, and began trying to evict the tenants. The city of New York had approved Sunday ball in 1920, and the Giants wanted as many of those lucrative dates as possible.

Squatters with an attitude, the Yankees won another pennant in 1922, with Ruth hitting only 35 homers in 110 games because of suspensions for off-season barnstorming and then for brawling. The Yankees lost the Series to the Giants again, but in the meantime, the Yankee owners were financing a new stadium in the Bronx, across the Harlem River, in plain sight of the Polo Grounds. Yankee Stadium opened in 1923 with the Yankees playing the Red Sox. Harry Frazee was an honored guest—and why not, given the great gift the Red Sox owner had bestowed on the Yankees? He didn't have that far to come, anyway, since his offices were in midtown Manhattan. Ruth hit a home run and Fred Lieb, a prominent New York sportswriter, called the place "The House That Ruth Built," a nickname that has stuck.

In 1925, Lou Gehrig, a strapping young first baseman out of Columbia University, became the perfect complement to Ruth. By the time they humbled Pittsburgh in the 1927 World Series, the Yankees were the dominant team in baseball.

Ruth and Gehrig were polar opposites. Gehrig was loyal, went home every evening to his wife, was not highly demanding to the owners (and thereby underpaid), while Ruth was still insubordinate and occasionally unhealthy. He missed part of the 1925 season after being taken off a train due to an illness still alluded to as a stomachache from too many hot dogs and soda but more likely the result of other excesses.

Ruth and Gehrig barnstormed together in the off-season, with the Babe willing to wear any hat handed to him—a classic clown, an instinctive showman, always generous to children. The country loved him. He also barnstormed as far away as Japan, now a baseball-mad nation, which cheered the visiting idol, Babu Rutu.

Together for 10 full seasons, from 1925 through 1934, they formed the most powerful one-two punch in baseball history, but their time was short. Ruth was phased out by the Yankees after 1934 and tried playing with the Boston Braves, hitting three home runs in Pittsburgh and almost immediately retiring on that last loud note. He then waited for the managing job with the Yankees, which, he eventually realized, was never going to come.

Gehrig's life took a far more disastrous turn. In the spring of 1939, he was diagnosed with a rare degenerative neuromuscular disease: amyotrophic lateral sclerosis (ALS), now called Lou Gehrig's disease. Upon his return from the Mayo Clinic in Minnesota, the Yankees held a ceremony for him between games of the July 4 doubleheader, with Ruth and many of his old teammates present. Gehrig wrote his own speech and delivered it to the huge crowd:

"For the past two weeks, you've been reading about a bad break," he said, pausing for a moment, the echoes resounding around the stadium. "Today I consider myself the luckiest man on the face of the earth." The stoic captain then recited all his blessings, including just about everybody from his parents to the concessionaires. It was perhaps the most emotional moment ever experienced in a ballpark; Gary Cooper, in the subsequent film *Pride of the Yankees,* could barely do justice to Gehrig's uncharacteristic baring of his emotions. The illness would kill Gehrig in twenty-three months.

Ruth, horrified by the death of his very dissimilar teammate, was close to a reformed man, with a second marriage and an adopted daughter. He had upgraded his table manners and learned to write letters, make speeches, and go out in public, and he still reveled in the glory of being the Babe whenever he visited a ballpark. His time, too, was short, as he was diagnosed with cancer. Other dying men, like the modest Gehrig, might make one public farewell performance. The Babe made three, the last one a few weeks before his death in August of 1948.

The early demise of both No. 3 and No. 4 set a melancholy mood that still hunkers under the eaves in Yankee Stadium, with its retired numbers and monuments to its own immortals—Mickey Mantle, Roger Maris, Billy Martin, Thurman Munson, Elston Howard, all of whom died way too young.

Years later, other players would surpass Ruth's home run totals, but he is still revered for his grandiose skills and flair, best described by the highly American adjective for prodigious: Ruthian.

—

The Babe was also kept alive by a second legend, baseball's own tale of two cities, with its overtones of prejudice and deceit. The villain in the Ruth saga is reputed to be Harry Frazee, the New York impresario who had sold Ruth to the Yankees. People have long since forgotten the ugly feud between Frazee and Ban Johnson, the league president, who controlled a majority of clubs known as the "Loyal Five," and opposed the owners of the Yankees, Red Sox, and White Sox, known as the "Insurrectos."

After Frazee bought the Sox from Joseph Lannin in 1916, Johnson referred to him as "the champion wrecker of baseball," because Frazee had sold key players to the Yankees. Frazee insisted that other league owners would not deal with him, so he had no choice but to deal with the two Yankee owners, whom he knew from New York. The two Yankee owners also helped Frazee take out a loan of $350,000 to secure his mortgage on Fenway Park, thereby putting them in line to own the Red Sox park.

The feud went deeper than that. Johnson was a Midwesterner who had primitive blue-state, red-state issues with New York and Boston. At the very least, Johnson found Frazee brash, perhaps because of his involvement in show business, which in some circles was regarded as a milieu in which no gentleman would ever participate. Johnson and his faithful owners often suggested Frazee was too "New York," which then and now could be taken as a code phrase for being Jewish.

The suggestion of anti-Semitism came from a familiar source of bigotry. Henry Ford of the automobile empire had founded a weekly newspaper, the *Dearborn Independent*, and used it to print allegations of sinister Jewish activity in America. In 1921, Ford's lead writer, J. Cameron, wrote an essay called "Jewish Gamblers Corrupt American Baseball," which focused on Arnold Rothstein of New York rather than on the players and other gamblers involved in the Black Sox plot. At the time, the *Independent* printed over 250,000 copies, all over the country and overseas.

Ford soon published another essay called "Jewish Degradation of American Baseball," zeroing in on Frazee: "Baseball was about as much of a sport to Frazee as selling tickets to a merry-go-round would be. He wanted to put his team across as if they were May Watson's girly-girly burlesquers." Cameron then called Jews "scavengers" who meant to turn baseball into "garbage." Cameron continued: "But there is no doubt anywhere, among either friends or critics of baseball, that the root cause of the present condition is due to Jewish influence. . . . If baseball is to be saved, it must be taken out of their hands."

Frazee was also denigrated by Fred Lieb, the prolific New York sportswriter who was a close friend of Ban Johnson. According to Glenn Stout, a New England–based writer, Lieb suggested Frazee's acts could be explained by his birth, while never exactly claiming Frazee was Jewish.

"We have been maligned," Frazee's great-grandson, Max Frazee, a New York–based construction official and artist, would say in 2004. The great-grandson was aghast at the bigotry of Henry Ford and others but he wanted to set the record straight: Harry Frazee was an Episcopalian of Scottish ancestry. Apparently being a New York was enough to qualify Frazee as Jewish, back in those days.

Generations of writers, including myself, have charged that Frazee sold Ruth to finance a Broadway musical called *No, No, Nanette*. As Glenn Stout has recently clarified, Frazee sold Ruth in January of 1920, three years before that show was even written. While his dealings with the Red Sox were questionable, Frazee was not destitute, as is sometimes suggested. When he died in 1929, his value was believed to be around $1.5 million.

Still, Frazee's reputation was forever ruined, first by the anti-Semitic insinuations and then by the continued failures of the Red Sox. Bereft of their best players, replenished by fading Yankee rejects, the Sox stumbled through the 1920s and 1930s. They would win four pennants but lost the World Series in 1946, 1967, 1975, and 1986, usually under excruciating circumstances.

When the Red Sox took a lead in the 1986 World Series, I took a cue from nervous Boston fans and wrote a column in the *New York Times* ("The Curse of Babe Ruth") anticipating the horrors that might befall the Sox in the sixth game. Sure enough, Bill Buckner had Mookie Wilson's ground ball trickle between his rickety ankles and the Sox went on to blow the entire Series. In a subsequent book, *The Curse of the Bambino*, Dan Shaughnessy of the *Boston Globe* would present his own cosmic theories about the ongoing spell over the Red Sox. From then on, every time the Red Sox would falter, Harry Frazee would be blamed.

VIII

MR. RICKEY

On June 28, 1907, a sore-armed third-string catcher with the New York Highlanders allowed the Washington Nationals to steal 13 bases in a single game. This major league record, still standing nearly a century later, is a representative bit of trivia that can be brought up at the ballpark when runners are stealing on some hapless receiver. Impress your neighbors! Share your obscure nugget of information! In a discussion of chicken-winged catchers, come up with the hallowed name of Branch Rickey!

"Rickey threw so poorly to bases that all a man had to do to put through a steal was to start," the *Washington Post* observed the next day.

Known at first for his college education and observance of the Sabbath, Rickey would play only 119 games in the major leagues, his days as innovator far ahead of him. Yet even then he was preparing for the cerebral side of the game, as opposed to the physical. He was sitting on the bench or spending time in the bullpen, warming up pitchers, but all the time Branch Wesley Rickey was thinking. He would become the forerunner of many hallowed baseball men who could not hit the broad side of a barn with a shovel—managers like Walter Alston, Sparky Anderson, Earl Weaver, and Gene Mauch, who learned the game by observing, via osmosis, through the seat of their pants.

Rickey went beyond managing, becoming baseball's da Vinci, the man who thought of many things. He became the very American face and voice of the game's eternal duality—rural vs. urban, crass vs. pious, corporal vs. mental. A man of the nineteenth century, he was the ancestor of twenty-first-century baseball, which blares patriotic anthems and then bombards the customers' eardrums with commercials.

Long after Rickey's death in 1965, his old players and staff members still referred to him as Mr. Rickey, still recalled his spring training lectures, still employed his theories and techniques, still quoted him ("addition by subtraction" or "luck is the residue of design"). For that matter, elderly ballplayers still shuddered when they recalled Rickey's cigar-fumed office—known to sportswriters as the Cave of the Winds—and Rickey's bushy eyebrows and jowly cheeks and biblical-driven explanations why he could not possibly spare another hundred dollars on their contract.

The psalm-quoting capitalist permanently changed the game with his inquisitive (and some would say acquisitive) mind, creating the first extensive farm system in the 1920s and hiring the first black major-leaguer of the century, Jackie Robinson, in the 1947 season. Rickey touched the careers of so many immortal players (George Sisler, Stan Musial, Jackie Robinson, Roberto Clemente) that sometimes it seems nobody could possibly have been in that many places. His rumpled suits and ornate speech provide the ageless American facade of this sport. Nowadays there are thirty-somethings running ball clubs, wearing jeans, strumming guitars, utilizing computers, and more power to them, but the face of the game remains an elderly gent, quoting Socrates or Moses, all the while listening to the turnstiles clang.

Mr. Rickey was not exactly Abe Lincoln, who emerged from a log cabin to become president, but Rickey's life does resonate from another place and time. He was a farm boy from southern Ohio who attended Ohio Wesleyan University and then joined the minor leagues, promising his mother that he would never work on Sunday, to honor their Christian beliefs. Rickey made it to the major leagues with the St. Louis Browns and New York Highlanders from 1905 through 1907, later playing two games back with the Browns in 1914.

His strength would be teaching and scouting, finding better ways to play the game. While still in the minor leagues, he had coached at his old school, Ohio Wesleyan, using football techniques to train his baseball players.

While earning a law degree and coaching at the University of Michigan in 1911, Rickey made the first great discovery of his career, George Sisler, a stylish first baseman who would play 15 seasons and bat .340. In his early days, Sisler twice outpitched the great

Walter (Big Train) Johnson before concentrating on first base. After Sisler retired in 1930, Rickey called him "the greatest player that ever lived," which may have been an exaggeration—Babe Ruth was both a better hitter and pitcher—but understandably loyal all the same.

By 1913 Rickey was back managing the Browns, initiating new drills in spring training for players who had previously gone from winter sloth to rusty baseball mechanics on the first day of camp. Rickey's camps included handball to improve hand-eye coordination, batting cages, sliding pits, a running track, and daily lectures to reinforce techniques being taught on the field, much as he would do with three other major league teams later in his life.

In 1919 Rickey switched to the Cardinals, then the secondary team in St. Louis. Ahead of his time, as always, Rickey took a control-freak interest in all the details, even the Cardinals' uniforms in 1921, splashing a logo of two redbirds across the chest of the uniforms, an idea he had gotten from a design of a church decoration in St. Louis. He also began the first Knothole Gang, allowing children into games for free, to build a new generation of fans, which the Cardinals sorely needed.

With no money for spring training, the Cards trained at home in chilly Midwestern March. Rickey once had to resort to selling a rug from his own home to meet the bills. "That kind of thing drove me mad," Rickey once said about the Cardinals' poverty. "I pondered long on it, and finally concluded that, if we were too poor to buy, we would have to raise our own."

He decided to build a reserve system of minor league players, an idea that went back to Albert Spalding. The minors had essentially remained independent, with clubs developing their own talent and selling it upward to the majors, at prices too high for the Cardinals. In 1919 Rickey began his empire by buying 18 percent of the Houston team in the Texas League, followed by a share of Fort Smith, Arkansas, in the Western Association. He loaded up the teams with the help of talent scouts, including Charlie Barrett, known as "the king of the weeds."

A national agreement of 1921 forbade major league clubs from stockpiling players, but some teams got around it by calling it "lending." In 1922, the United States Supreme Court heard a complaint by the Baltimore team from the upstart Federal League, alleging that the major leagues illegally wielded a reserve clause on players, in restraint of free trade and in violation of the Sherman Act of 1890.

Chief Justice Oliver Wendell Holmes delivered an opinion for the unanimous majority that baseball did not constitute interstate commerce. "The business is giving exhibitions of baseball, which are purely state affairs," wrote Justice Holmes, who added, "Owners produce baseball games as a source of profit, [they] cannot change the character of the games. They are still sport, not trade."

That opinion would strengthen club owners for more than half a century, handing them legal control of their players, whose only options were to accept the contract offered them or not play at all. By defining baseball as a sport, the Supreme Court had essentially turned it into a national asset. It was bad enough that the general public accepted this pro-business decision, but many players came to believe it, too. They smarted under arbitrary salary limits, but at the same time resisted calls to collective action, as if unionism were a treasonous act against their homeland. A good portion of the sporting press went along with it, too.

Empowered by the Supreme Court's decision, Rickey continued to buy up portions of minor league teams, along with the contracts of hundreds of players. Unsuccessful at managing, Rickey was replaced in 1925 by Rogers Hornsby, the great second baseman. With Rickey concentrating on the front office, the Cardinals won their first pennant in 1926 and beat the Yankees in the World Series, with Grover Cleveland Alexander trekking out of the bullpen to save the seventh game, while he was allegedly hungover. By 1928, the Cardinals had five farm teams, and fifty of their former farmhands were in the major leagues.

Rickey's stockpile soon caught the attention of Judge Landis, who liberated approximately 100 minor-leaguers from their contracts, unleashing the phrase "Rickey's chain gang." Rickey was unabashed. "He would go to places like South Dakota, North Dakota,

Iowa, and pay a certain figure to every club for the rights to the best player on the roster," said his grandson, Branch B. Rickey, who in 2005 was the president of the Pacific Coast League.

The Cardinals also won pennants in 1928, 1930, 1931, and 1934, as Rickey constantly reloaded his dynasty with players like the loquacious Jay Hanna (Dizzy) Dean, out of Lucas, Arkansas, who won 58 games in 1934–35. With the Depression gripping the land in the 1930s, Rickey's scouts recruited in areas suffering from poverty and desperation—coming up with Albert (Red) Schoendienst from Germantown, Illinois, who had suffered an eye injury while training in the Civilian Conservation Corps; Stanley Frank Musial, from smogbound Donora, Pennsylvania; Enos Slaughter from Roxboro, North Carolina.

Long after his fabled dash home to win the 1946 World Series, Slaughter reminisced how he had been signed by Wanzer Rickey, the brother of Branch and apparently very much from the same frugal mold. Slaughter said Wanzer had given him a modest signing bonus of a shotgun and two hunting dogs, but the two dogs had run away almost immediately. The funny thing was, Slaughter added, that Dizzy Dean had an identical signing experience with the Cardinals many years earlier. "Me and Diz always wondered if they were the same two dogs," Slaughter said.

At first, Rickey's empire-building methods were scorned by John J. McGraw, who, for the record, had also scoffed at Babe Ruth's home runs. In turn, the Yankees were slow to build a farm system but on November 12, 1931, Jacob Ruppert purchased the Newark, New Jersey, team just across the Hudson River, and stocked it up with Yankee farmhands. The Yankees managed to have it both ways, rolling through the 1930s by signing young stars like Joe DiMaggio and Tony Lazzeri from strong independent teams in the Pacific Coast League and elsewhere.

Rickey gave the impression of having taken a vow of poverty, but the poverty seemed to apply mostly to his players. By the end of his time with the Cardinals, his salary was said to be $75,000, plus a percentage of the price every time the Cardinals sold a player. Those terms do not sound like much this age when general managers make multimillion-dollar rock-star salaries, but Rickey's income during the Depression was considerable, particularly for an executive who could quote the Sermon on the Mount to players asking for a raise.

According to legend, Rickey balanced the sacred and the secular, observing the Sabbath while keeping both eyes on the turnstiles. On Sundays he rented a room in the YMCA across from Sportsman's Park, training binoculars on the ticket lines. He preached ethical behavior but his Cardinals were called the Gashouse Gang because of their rough ways. They committed pranks in hotels, played Dixieland on banjos and harmonicas during long train rides, fought with the opposition or amongst themselves—and won pennants.

Shortly after the Cardinals won the pennant in 1942, the Cardinals' owner, Sam Breadon, said he could no longer afford Rickey. Moving on to Brooklyn, Rickey continued to stockpile and train young talent, particularly in spring training. In 1948, the Dodgers bought a former naval air base in Vero Beach, Florida, eventually calling it Dodgertown. Amidst the barracks and diamonds, Rickey was in his glory, personally delivering lectures on subjects like "The Cure Is Sweat" and "Leisure Time Is the Anathema of Youth." He imposed rules on his players, many of them veterans of combat in World War Two—no cards, no liquor, no cigarettes, frequent weight checks, backed up by refusals of second helpings at the base cafeteria.

He also introduced the first pitching machines plus a contraption of strings, the size of a strike zone, to teach pitchers control without the embarrassment of an umpire, batter, and watchful fans. Many a wild young pitcher, including Sandy Koufax, was taken out behind the barracks to pitch to the strings.

For a religious man, Rickey was something of a conniver, known to leave fake contracts conveniently in view on his desk, intimidating his players by making them think the pay scale was even lower than they had imagined. More than half a century later, Rickey's frugality still rankled Ralph Branca, who had been the Dodgers' best pitcher in 1947. "I won 21 games," Branca recalled in 2005, "and I led the league in starts with 36, but he told me I walked too many batters. Yeah, I walked 98—because I pitched 280 innings. I sent the contract back. He was mad at me."

Rickey's time in Brooklyn came to an end in 1950, when he was pushed out by the new owner, Walter O'Malley. Rickey's teaching methods did not work with the destitute Pirates and he left after 1955. Half a century later, Branch B. Rickey reminisced about the old-fashioned life at the Rickey farm outside Pittsburgh. "We were not country-club," the grandson said proudly, recalling the pungent odor of the livestock. The center of family life was the Sabbath midday dinner. "I can see my grandfather at the head of the table, anywhere from six to fourteen people," the grandson said. "He liked to have out-of-towners, make them comfortable. It caused us to have dialogues mixed with social dialogues."

In 1960, Rickey tried to build a rival league, the Continental League, which never got off the ground but did force the first expansion of the majors. He then had a brief role as advisor to the Cardinals' ownership in 1964, apparently trying to get his old accomplice, Leo Durocher, hired to replace the fatherly manager, Johnny Keane.

As a young reporter in 1964, I got a glimpse of Rickey on the night the Cardinals surged into first place during a fantastic pennant race. We were in Keane's tiny office when a hidden door suddenly opened and beetle-browed, three-piece-suited Branch Rickey materialized, like Banquo's Ghost.

"Johnny Keane, you're a gosh-dang good manager!" Rickey thundered at the man he had been undermining for months. Then Rickey was gone. Keane won the World Series—and immediately quit the Cardinals to join the Yankees.

A year later, Rickey collapsed at a banquet in his honor, and he died soon afterward, just short of eighty-four. In essence, baseball's great teacher went out talking.

IX

THE NEGRO LEAGUES

While seeking talent for the Cardinals in the destitute corners of the country, Branch Rickey was not ready to tap one great source of talent: black America. Baseball had remained white since the late nineteenth century, when Albert Spalding and Cap Anson contrived to keep blacks out; it preached about being the national pastime and received special dispensation from Congress and the courts, yet it remained segregated nearly halfway into the next century.

Black players got the message, and formed teams of their own. In 1885, in Babylon, Long Island, New York, a headwaiter at the Argyle Hotel named Frank Thompson organized a team of waiters, called the Cuban Giants. In order to get white fans to ignore their dark skins, the players pretended to speak Spanish, correctly assuming that hardly anybody in the United States could tell they were actually speaking gibberish. The novelty helped the waiters become full-time touring players, with white owners backing them up. Sometimes the players livened up their games with comedy routines—jokes, songs, snappy games of catch with exaggerated motions, maybe a pitcher telling his fielders to sit down while he handled the batter by himself. With their flair for show business, the Cuban Giants were the forerunners of other black teams that felt the need to entertain, like the Harlem Globetrotters of basketball. Just like black actors or singers or even public figures of the day, they had to seem simple, innocent, and harmless.

Blacks also played the game straight. In 1887, the National Colored Base Ball League, the first attempt at a professional Negro League, was formed. Rebuffed by white America, blacks formed touring teams that played in ramshackle stadiums in black neighborhoods, or sometimes in rented big-league stadiums, producing players now recognized as the equal of the greatest white players, including Josh Gibson, Buck Leonard, and Satchel Paige.

Sometimes players slipped through to the major leagues, often

Cuban players ostensibly of Spanish heritage. The darker the skin, the louder the insults. A few players of mixed race undoubtedly managed to pass as white or Native American. In my home I have a coffee-table book containing photographs of various major league players from the past ten decades. In the section from the 1920s, a rather inconspicuous player from a border state has noticeably mixed features. My guess is that this player had passed the color scrutiny and was able to earn a major league salary for a few years—and more power to him.

Generally, it was not easy for a player to get past the vigilant race detectors. John J. McGraw, in his last year with Baltimore in 1901, tried to hire Charlie Grant, a bellhop at the Orioles' spring training base in Arkansas, to play the infield, as long as Grant would maintain the fiction that he was of Cherokee ancestry. After Charles Comiskey threatened to sign a "Chinaman" for his White Sox, the furor ended McGraw's plans. Charlie Grant remained a bellhop until the day he died.

Rumors persisted that Babe Ruth was part black, based partially on his athletic skills and partially on his broad, flat nose. There was absolutely no basis to this urban legend. In one famous family photograph taken in fin de siècle Baltimore, young George Herman Ruth looks just like dozens of his relatives gathered on a classic white stoop. Nevertheless, many blacks bragged on Ruth, who, while typically congenial to blacks, observed the normal racist language of the day. The great Bambino would accept "monkey" and "ape" as normal heckling from the opposing bench jockeys but would threaten to fight opponents who used racial slurs on him. "Don't get personal," the Babe warned.

Some American blacks migrated to Cuba early in the century, relishing the chance to play against touring major league teams like the Tigers, Giants, and Athletics. The aptly named Ban Johnson was so upset when the A's divided eight games, many against the star Cuban pitcher Jose Mendez, that he prohibited his teams from visiting the island. "We want no makeshift club calling themselves the Athletics to go to Cuba to be beaten by colored teams," Johnson said. Ty Cobb and McGraw uttered the same sour grapes after humbling trips to Cuba.

In 1911, Andrew (Rube) Foster, a tall pitcher out of Texas, formed his own team, the Chicago American Giants, or Foster's Giants, as people called them. Foster was an astute businessman with ties to the white community, once helping to rebuild the grandstand at the White Sox' South Side ballpark, where his players were welcome only as tenants, not equals.

Four years later, Foster challenged the upstart Federal League to admit his team but was turned down. He waited out the war and the gambling scandal of 1919, and then in 1920 Foster lobbied for admission of black players to the major leagues. He was led to understand this was not a priority of Judge Landis.

Realizing that blacks would have to play in a parallel universe, Foster helped organize the Negro National League in 1920, with eight teams, mostly in the Midwest. He felt strongly that the ownership should be black, but he did accept J. L. Wilkinson, the white owner of the powerful Kansas City Monarchs, who helped keep Negro baseball alive. Shortly after that came the Negro Southern League and the Eastern Colored League. In 1924, the first Negro World Series was played, with the Monarchs beating the Hilldale Daisies from Darby, Pennsylvania, five games to four.

In the fall, the Negro teams barnstormed with white players, doing so well that in 1921 Judge Landis ordered all white stars to not wear their major league uniforms while playing black teams. In 1926, Foster suffered a nervous breakdown and his league began a quick downturn. He died in 1930 and the league disbanded in 1931, while the Eastern League had disbanded in 1927.

Still, Negro baseball thrived, partially because of the energy from one city—Pittsburgh. The first powerhouse was the Homestead Grays, representing a steel town on the Monongahela River, just south of Pittsburgh, once the base of a giant United States Steel plant.

The Grays were founded in 1912 by Cumberland Posey, a black athlete who had attended Penn State. He kept his team out of the

Negro Leagues because he rightfully felt he could make more money playing an independent schedule, going where the money was, two or three games a day, and sometimes picking up the best players from other teams for cameo performances.

Money was tight during the Depression, but one industry in which blacks could participate was the numbers, the illegal lottery system with winners, losers, and runners on every corner. Gus Greenlee, who ran the Pittsburgh operation, did so well that in 1930 he took over the Pittsburgh Crawfords, a black team from the Hill District. Greenlee spent $100,000 to build his own stadium near his Crawford Bar and Grille, known for its food, music, and good times.

In short order, Greenlee accumulated five players who would one day be initiated into the Baseball Hall of Fame: Josh Gibson, Satchel Paige, Oscar Charleston, Judy Johnson, and Cool Papa Bell. Gibson was born in Georgia but his father moved to Pittsburgh to work in the Carnegie-Illinois Steel Plant. The young man dropped out of school after the fifth grade to work in the mills and became a promising catcher at the age of nineteen. In 1930, the Grays' catcher, Buck Ewing, split a finger while catching a Sunday double-header against the touring Monarchs. The Grays sent across town for Gibson, who was playing against a white team, and he caught the second game. He was soon a legend, known as "Sampson." Greenlee's wad of bills soon recruited Gibson to the Crawfords.

In 1933, Greenlee and his colleagues organized one of the great events in Negro League baseball, the East-West Game, which drew 20,000 fans to Comiskey Park, named after the white pioneer who had blown the whistle on the "Cherokee" bellhop, Charlie Grant. The White Sox gained an annual big rent day, as the all-star game became a highlight of the calendar for blacks, not only for the high level of baseball but also for the style of the celebrities who flocked to Chicago. With the Depression putting millions of people out of work, the Negro Leagues became one of the most important black industries in the country.

Cumberland Posey got the message from his rival, Greenlee, and in 1935 he entered his Grays in the Negro National League. In

1937, Posey enticed Gibson back to the Grays to play alongside Buck Leonard, the first baseman, forming one of the great tandems in baseball history, comparable to Ruth and Gehrig. The Grays would win nine consecutive Negro National League championships and three Negro World Series titles.

Gibson is said to have hit more home runs than Babe Ruth or Henry Aaron, and longer, too. Witnesses said he once hit a fair ball out of Yankee Stadium, which has never been accomplished in a Yankee game, not by Ruth, or even Mickey Mantle, who came close. He is given credit for 84 home runs in 1936, including 200 league and barnstorming games, not necessarily all against the top level of Negro League teams.

Leonard was often called "the Black Lou Gehrig," except, his fans insisted, the doomed captain of the Yankees could very well have been called "the White Buck Leonard." Oscar Charleston was a left-handed hitting outfielder who played for half a dozen teams and is often mentioned as the best Negro League hitter, ever.

The Grays played home games at Forbes Field, the home of the Pittsburgh Pirates, but also used Griffith Stadium, in Washington, D.C., as a home field. The Griffith family, just like the Comiskey family, managed to make money by keeping blacks out of the majors.

It is sad to think about the lost careers, the failed chances for great athletes to make a good living and prove themselves. Yet Negro League baseball was not gloomy when Satchel Paige fixed his deadpan mother-wit stare on the batter and extended his huge left foot high in the air and delivered his vast assortment of pitches, one of which he called "the bee" because it buzzed. The sense of deprivation was temporarily forgotten when Cool Papa Bell ran so fast that it was said he once hit himself with his own line drive while sliding into second base. It might have happened.

Not tied into the rigid methods of the major leagues, the black players and their leaders had the freedom to experiment. The Monarchs carried a portable lighting system for night games, allowing them to play two and three games a day. Most Negro teams played a very serious brand of ball but a few, like the Indianapolis

Clowns, perfected routines to entertain the crowd—whipping the ball around the infield, sometimes playing "shadow ball," which included imaginary diving catches in the outfield.

The best baseball of all was probably played in October, after the major leagues' season had ended and the major-leaguers augmented their salaries by barnstorming. Dizzy Dean used to proclaim the greatest pitcher he had ever seen was "that old colored boy—Satchel Paige." Most of the white major-leaguers, except for hard-core bigots like Ty Cobb, admitted their autumn opponents were their equals. Nevertheless, Paige and Gibson were still unknown to the average white fan.

According to most records, the Negro League stars held a margin of 309–129 over the major-leaguers in documented barnstorm games. The dominance can be explained partially by motivation but also because Negro players had developed their own style based on speed, surprise, and mental alertness. "In games between white and black all-star teams, this style of play often confounded the major leaguers," Jules Tygiel has written. "Centerfielder Cool Papa Bell personified this approach. In one game against a major league all-star squad, Bell scored from first base on a sacrifice bunt."

———

Negro League players were also innovators of equipment. Pepper Bassett, famed for an occasional catching stint in a cut-down rocking chair, removed the padding from his bulky mitt to create a more flexible modern glove. After Willie Wells of the Newark Eagles was hit in the head by Bill Byrd of the Baltimore Elite Giants in 1942, he plopped a workman's hardhat on his head the next time he faced Byrd.

Some teams were reflections of the high standards and high hopes of the Negro community. In New Jersey, Effa Manley (who said she was white but lived among blacks) ran the Newark Eagles for her husband, Abe, a major numbers banker. Employing her potent mix of brains, beauty, and will, Manley prepared her talented players like Monte Irvin, Larry Doby, and Don Newcombe for the day the major leagues would come calling. Of course, when the majors did open up, they did not pay Manley for the investment and care she had provided.

Other players did not stick around the States to wait for that day. Willie Wells played in Mexico for many years. In 1944, Wells told Wendell Smith, the distinguished columnist for the *Pittsburgh Courier,* "I am not faced by the racial problem. . . . I've found freedom and democracy here, something I never found in the United States. . . . In Mexico I am a man."

———

In 1942, the last Negro League World Series was held, with the Kansas City Monarchs beating the Crawfords in four straight games. War was coming. Money was drying up. Once Jackie Robinson and others joined the major leagues in 1947, the Negro Leagues were doomed.

The Homestead Grays disbanded after the 1950 season while the touring teams hobbled on for a few more years. Virtually forgotten for decades, the Grays and their opponents are now coming into their own. In July of 2002, Allegheny County and Homestead borough officials changed the name of a 3,000-foot-long bridge to the Homestead Grays Bridge.

Half a century after their demise, the Negro Leagues are part of a proud folklore, with many of their players voted into the Baseball Hall of Fame, many of them posthumously, many of them without ever playing in the majors. Gibson, an alcoholic, died of a stroke in 1946 at the age of thirty-five. Buck Leonard was too old when the majors opened up in 1947. Oscar Charleston would find himself stranded on third base, overqualified in a AAA league, held back by unspoken quotas, watching younger blacks move past him to reach the majors. One swing, Charleston used to say. All he wanted was one swing in the majors. He never got it, although late in life he would be voted into the Hall of Fame.

Once banned from roadside diners, forced to take leftover dates in major stadiums, ignored by mainstream America, the Negro League teams are now admired retroactively: a trendy fashion note as well as a sign of defiance or homage. One can walk down a street in any major city and see somebody, not necessarily black, wearing the garb of the Pittsburgh Crawfords or the Homestead Grays, purchased in high-end sporting goods shops or hawked online, and not cheap, either. Major League Baseball now recognizes the Negro Leagues by selling their gear. In 1995, MLB coughed up the first profits from selling imitation Negro League memorabilia, checks worth $143,248 for survivors and family members.

At the very least, the retro Crawfords and the faux Grays send a message of nostalgia and regret. Parents may have to explain to their children how Josh Gibson once hit homers as far and as frequently as Babe Ruth and Henry Aaron, but an admirer of Josh Gibson walks down Michigan Avenue, in a fashionable jacket. After decades of segregation, it seems only fair.

X

RADIO DAYS

In August of 1921, one of the great American combinations was unveiled—even better than the peanut butter and jelly sandwich. This fortuitous new blend was radio and baseball.

Up to then, baseball had been available only to people who went out to the ballpark or congregated around a telegraph set for the results of a World Series game or read the results in the sports pages, a contribution from William Randolph Hearst's newspaper empire back in 1885.

But starting in 1921, baseball began providing almost instant pitch-by-pitch information to fans in kitchens, offices, living rooms, saloons, and eventually cars. Radio also created that reassuring, loopy American presence, the hometown broadcaster.

The first game was broadcast by Harold Arlin, a twenty-six-year-old technician with radio station KDKA in Pittsburgh, on August 5, 1921. Using a microphone cobbled together from a converted telephone, he re-created the pitch-by-pitch details clattering over the Western Union wire, via Morse code. From his perch a few miles from the ballpark, he also improvised some fanciful details.

"I was just a nobody, and our broadcast—back then, at least—wasn't that big a deal," Arlin said in 1984, two years before his death at ninety. "Our guys at KDKA didn't even think that baseball would last on radio. I did it sort of as a one-shot project, a kind of addendum to the events we'd already done."

Two months later, the first game of the 1921 World Series between the Giants and Yankees was also broadcast on KDKA, as well as WJZ in Newark, New Jersey, and WBZ in Springfield, Massachusetts. Grantland Rice, the famous sports columnist, was broadcasting live inside the Polo Grounds while another broadcaster took the pitch-by-pitch details from the telegraph signals.

Within a decade, most baseball towns, major and minor—except, surprisingly, New York—were enlivened by the warbling or staccato voices of men (always men) describing baseball games. At first, most broadcasts were a new art form—baseball from the clickety-clack of the telegraph, helped immeasurably by the man in the studio.

One local announcer, Ronald (Dutch) Reagan, honed his vivid imagination while describing Chicago Cubs games, despite the theoretical handicap of his being in a studio in Des Moines, Iowa. Reagan later moved to Hollywood and became first an actor and then governor of California and later president of the United States.

To cover up a malfunction in the telegraph system, broadcasters were adept at inventing reasons for the interruption: arguments at home plate, grave injuries, sudden rain squalls, swarms of locusts, anything to explain a break in the action. But imagination was not checked when games began to be broadcast from the ballpark. These flights of fantasy troubled the newspaper reporters who shared the same sardine-can press boxes.

"I don't know which game to write about—the one I saw today, or the one I heard Graham McNamee announce as I sat next to him at the Polo Grounds," Ring Lardner wrote.

Eventually, the electronic and print sections of the press boxes were separated by soundproof panels, so the writers would not be distracted by the version going out over the airwaves. Up to that point, writers had been kings of the sports media, but their status began plummeting downward and has never recovered.

All broadcasters developed their own styles, nervous twitches, verbal tics. Generally unseen, they were Everyman, with spectacles and brimmed hats, straight out of Sinclair Lewis's *Main Street,* the best-selling novel of 1921. Curt Smith, a former White House speechwriter for George H. W. Bush, wrote a book, *Voices of the Game,* in which he described the appeal of Cincinnati's first popular broadcaster, Harry Hartman:

"Harry was sort of rough around the edges, it's true, and his dictionary wasn't too thick, but he was earthy and people liked him," said Lee Allen, a native of Cincinnati and later a historian at the Baseball Hall of Fame. "Please remember—southern Ohio's a very old-fashioned, cornball sort of place, 'Little Germany' and all that. Well, Harry was like that anyway, and he fit in."

Before long, every ball club had developed its very own dotty uncle, complete with signature phrases. "Get up, Aunt Minnie, and raise the window! Here she comes!" was the whoop by Rosey Rowswell, who broadcast Pirate games for KDKA from 1936 through 1954. As the Pirate home run cleared the fence, one of Rowswell's assistants would simulate a broken window or scattered pots and pans. "That's too bad," Rowswell would shout. "She tripped over a garden hose! Aunt Minnie never made it!"

Arch McDonald of WTOP in Washington, D.C., would shout, "There she goes, Mrs. Murphy!" at every home run by the Senators. Mel Allen of the Yankees would shout "How about that?" quite frequently.

The early broadcasters brought the game to the far corners of America, via 50,000-watt clear-channel stations, accessible in a dozen states. Fans in Arkansas and Georgia became fans of the St. Louis Cardinals via station KMOX. In dense valleys of Appalachia, fans picked up the games over WLIW in Cincinnati or KDKA in Pittsburgh. In rural sections of upstate New York, you could pick up games on several New York stations—or from Boston, Cleveland, Detroit.

If gravitas were the standard, Walter Lanier (Red) Barber was the first great baseball broadcaster. A Southerner, Barber had the ascetic dignity of a lay preacher, the education of a college graduate, and the code of an actual journalist. "He reminds me of the Arabian horse," said Buzzie Bavasi, the former Dodger executive. "Every thoroughbred racehorse in the world is descended from the Arabian. Every announcer learned something from Red."

Barber started college late, after working in the fields of central Florida, and he first spoke into a microphone on the University of Florida station only because somebody else failed to show up. In 1934, at the age of twenty-six, Barber was hired by the Cincinnati Reds' new owner, Powel Crosley, Jr., to broadcast games over the Crosley radio stations. The first major league baseball game he ever saw, he described.

He did fine, cultivating his own Faulknerian phrases, calling his perch in the radio booth the Catbird Seat, a phrase he learned from a poker player smugly holding the winning cards. What Irish people called a donnybrook, Barber called a rhubarb. To punctuate a rally-ending play, Barber tersely described the key details, then used the phase "Oh, doctor," before letting the crowd noise finish the story.

Barber's familiar "Oh, doctor" has since been appropriated by latter-day broadcasters, just as the exclamation "Holy cow!" has become the trademark of several broadcasters. The long and informal makeup of the sport continues to produce strange sound effects, including those from Chris Berman of ESPN, who is popular for his obsessive puns on players' names. Nobody breaks Aunt Minnie's dishes anymore.

———

Lighting was another major innovation that came about on Barber's watch, while he worked for the new Cincinnati general manager, Larry MacPhail, a Rickey protégé. While running the Cardinals' farm team in Columbus, Ohio, MacPhail had induced Depression-age fans to spend their remaining quarters on the Red Birds after he spruced up the ballpark, ran promotions, and installed lights to permit night games. Moving to Cincinnati, MacPhail decided to put in lights there, too. He saw the value in letting fans eat supper after a hard day at the factory, and then, as the Ohio River valley heat subsided, making their way toward shimmering lights on the western edge of downtown.

Dire results were predicted. Fans would go blind. Players would be maimed. Morals would tumble. Crimes would be committed.

The first major league night game was against the Phillies on May 24, 1935. President Franklin D. Roosevelt pressed a telegraph key, made of Alaskan gold, a gift to President William Howard Taft many years earlier, thereby turning on the lights in Cincinnati. The light towers, with their 632 bulbs, costing a total of $50,000, used up more than a million watts of electricity.

"They waited until it got good and dark," Barber recalled in 1988. "And then the lights came on at precisely 8:30 P.M. The crowd immediately became ecstatically happy, and the game itself was beautifully played."

The Reds' Paul Derringer beat the Phillies' Joe Bowman, 2–1. In 1988, Bowman recalled: "There was a lot of talk about how you weren't going to be able to see the ball, you'd only see half the ball, and so on. I didn't have any trouble seeing the ball."

Night games changed baseball forever. The players no longer had a regular schedule of sleeping or eating and had more excuse to become night owls, but many fans welcomed the lower temperatures at night. For baseball writers, with first-edition deadlines looming in the early evening, there was now the need to come up with a story before the game, putting more attention on issues and personalities, rather than the play-by-play details.

MacPhail moved on to Brooklyn, where he installed a set of lights for the first night game on June 15, 1938. A large crowd was more attracted by the lights than the young Cincinnati starting pitcher, Johnny Vander Meer, who had pitched a no-hitter in his previous start. Under the new lights, Vander Meer walked eight men but pitched his second consecutive no-hitter. No other pitcher has ever done it.

The critics of night games tended to be won over by the sound of turnstiles. After seeing fans surge into the first night game in Washington, Clark Griffith, the owner of the team, began campaigning to raise baseball's temporary limit from seven to twenty-one night games. One by one, the major league teams installed lights, until 1948, when fifteen of sixteen teams had them.

The last holdout for day games would be dear old Wrigley Field. The ownership resisted until 1988 when the Cubs were battling for a postseason berth and the networks pointed out the differing income between day playoff games and night playoff games. Despite great gnashing of teeth from traditionalists, Commissioner Peter Ueberroth, a man with respect for the bottom line, ordered the Cubs to put in lights.

By 1990, 71 percent of major league games were scheduled at 5:00 P.M. or later. (The doubleheader, that old staple, was virtually gone.) A decade later, the figure of night games had dropped slightly to 67 percent. World Series games, however, were all played at night, at 8:00 or 8:30 P.M. on the East Coast, which meant that eastern television markets were essentially abandoning children. The networks said it made economic sense, and baseball capitulated, meanwhile brooding that children were more interested in video games than ball games.

In New York, all three teams resisted regular radio into the late 1930s, fearing broadcasting the games would cut into ticket sales. But in 1939, MacPhail brought Red Barber from Cincinnati to Brooklyn, and the other two New York teams had to compete. The Yankees brought in Arch McDonald from Washington, where he was known as "The Rembrandt of Re-creation," to work the Giant and Yankee home games. He lasted a year and was replaced by Mel Allen, with that mellifluous Southern voice that somehow worked so well in the Bronx.

—

The next logical leap from radio was television. The first televised game was on May 17, 1939, between Princeton and Columbia universities, broadcast by NBC, which used one camera. The broadcaster was Bill Stern, who was known for his apocryphal tales, including one that had Abraham Lincoln urging the Union troops to make the world safe for baseball. (In those inventive times, Stern was also known for changing football ball-carriers in the middle of a play, requiring a lot of sideways handoffs or passes. A colleague once explained why Stern might not be ideal for broadcasting horse races: "You can't lateral a horse.")

A few months later, Barber called the first game of a Saturday doubleheader between Cincinnati and Brooklyn for NBC. According to the *New York Times,* "Television set owners as far as fifty miles away viewed the action and heard the roar of the crowd."

After World War Two, the NBC network came up with *The Game of the Week,* with a phalanx of broadcasters, producers, and statisticians descending on one chosen game. "As a kid growing up, there wasn't a lot for me to do in Searchlight," Senator Harry Reid, the Democrat minority leader, said in 2005 about his childhood in rural Nevada. "No parks. No high school. No movie theater." Reid added: "But we did have our radios and the baseball *Game of the*

Week. I looked forward to this broadcast, and even remember the disappointment I felt after I tuned in some afternoons, only to hear it was raining in some far-off city and there would be no game that day. The radio brought some of the greatest names in baseball to Searchlight, including Jackie Robinson and his Brooklyn Dodger teammates."

Meanwhile, local broadcasters babbled on, with homespun familiarity, attuned to every nuance from the first day of spring training. Ernie Harwell from Georgia, more Barber than Allen, brought his Southern lilt first to New York before finding his destiny in Detroit. The Midwest had a grand postwar collection of Jack Buck in St. Louis, Bob Prince in Pittsburgh, and Harry Caray, who moved from St. Louis to Chicago but remained the ultimate beery, beefy hometown rooter, shirtless on a muggy day, myopic despite dark framed glasses, sputtering "Take Me Out to the Ball Game" at the seventh-inning stretch.

The new major league towns built their own traditions. Vince Scully, who joined the Dodgers out of radio station WFUV at Fordham University, studied at the right hand of Red Barber. When the Dodgers moved to Los Angeles in 1958, fans carried transistor radios to the ballpark, which had never happened in the raucous confines of Ebbets Field, where fans did not need to be educated or entertained. In quiet moments in L.A., you could hear Scully's mellow voice, tutoring the nouveau fans in the subtleties of major league baseball—at least until the seventh inning, when the nouveau fans would depart, to beat the traffic jam.

Just as people try to quantify the "greatest ever" in various disciplines—Sugar Ray Robinson is the "greatest boxer ever, pound for pound," and so forth—so baseball fans argue over who was the best broadcaster ever. Scully often comes in first.

In 2005, Curt Smith came up with an arcane rating system in the book *Voices of Summer: Ranking Baseball's 101 All-Time Best Announcers.* Smith ranked Scully first, using terms like "nonpareil" and "Baseball's Olivier," which sound about right. Out of loyalty to my ancient Brooklyn Dodger childhood, I'd still go with Red Barber first, but Scully deserves all the kudos he gets. He has become a trifle slick and chirpy since moving to the Left Coast in 1958, but nobody calls a game like him, with wit and voice and knowledge.

Here is the quintessential Vince Scully, calling the 1980 post-season series between Houston and Philadelphia: In the fourth game, the Astros hit into a highly unusual double play on a fly ball to right field, followed by a relay to the pitcher and onward to the third baseman to catch a runner who had strayed too far off third base. As the music for the inning-ending commercial began to sound in the background, Scully summed it up quickly, using the scorecard symbols for the three participating fielders: *Just your basic nine-one-five double play,* Scully said, knowing that real baseball fans would understand the staccato eloquence of his call. Fade to commercial.

———

The first generation of broadcasters allowed fans to forget about the Depression, temporarily, at least, just as cheap movies got people out of the house, looking for cheap entertainment and maybe even the door prize of a free set of dishes. Baseball attendance fell after peaking at 10 million in 1930, and many owners lost money, with Connie Mack resorting to his old solution of selling off his best players.

One jolt of revenue and excitement came from an all-star game, first proposed by Arch Ward, the sports editor of the *Chicago Tribune,* who was trying to come up with a moneymaking sports event during Chicago's exposition in 1933. The first All-Star home run was hit, appropriately enough, by Babe Ruth. The All-Star Game had instant cachet as a novelty because the two rival leagues met only in spring training exhibitions and in the World Series.

The curious fans and players were rewarded by the 1934 All-Star Game, played in the Polo Grounds. Carl Hubbell, the angular screwball specialist with the Giants, struck out five consecutive sluggers who would one day be selected for the Hall of Fame—Babe Ruth, Lou Gehrig, and Jimmie Foxx to end the first inning and Al Simmons and Joe Cronin in the second. This is one of those career-defining baseball moments that can emerge from the timeless clarity of a scorecard. Three decades later, when Hubbell was a senior executive with the now San Francisco Giants, the back of his left hand would hang abnormally against his left pants pocket, the result of a career of throwing the screwball, a reverse curveball. Young reporters would nudge each other at the sight of the grizzled old lefty, as we thought about the day in 1934 when Hubbell struck out five Hall of Famers.

An injury in the 1937 All-Star Game led directly to the end of Dean's pitching career but the commencement of his new vocation as broadcaster, much to the chagrin of schoolteachers and grammarians. Ole Diz was not the first ballplayer to become a broadcaster: a former Cleveland outfielder, Jack Graney, had replaced the radio pioneer Tom Manning in 1932. But Dean soon brought his uninhibited Arkansas patois ("He slud into third") to the job.

Baseball had an infusion of new stars in the 1930s, including Rickey's pugnacious Cardinals, later known as the Gashouse Gang. The Cardinals were about to clinch the 1934 World Series when Detroit fans, angered by the hard-sliding Joe Medwick, began heaping fruit on him in left field. Judge Landis, knowing he would only make matters worse if he ruled a 9–0 forfeit against the Tigers, asked Medwick to leave the game for safety's sake, and the Cardinals wrapped up their championship.

Even after Ruth left after 1934, the Yankees dominated the American League, but the league had plenty of other stars, including Hank Greenberg from the Bronx, a powerful first baseman with Detroit, the first great Jewish star. In 1936, a seventeen-year-old pitcher, Bob Feller, joined Cleveland, straight from the farm in Van Meter, Iowa. That same year, Joe DiMaggio, a graceful and powerful center fielder, joined the Yankees. And in 1939, a rookie named Ted Williams, brash and brilliant, was dubbed "The Kid" by the older Red Sox.

Nineteen forty-one was epic for all three young stars. Feller led the league with 25 victories and 260 strikeouts while DiMaggio hit in 56 straight games, one of the sport's most enduring records, and Williams batted .406, the last time any hitter has surpassed .400.

Nobody will ever know what Hank Greenberg might have accomplished that season. With war breaking out in Europe and Asia, the United States began its first peacetime military draft in October of 1940, and the Tiger star was drafted in May of 1941. On May 6, Greenberg hit two homers against the Yankees. The next day he reported for military duty.

XI

WAR

In the terrible nights in the Pacific, when American and Japanese troops hunkered down in darkness only a few yards apart on the atolls and in the jungles, they hurled curses at one another. The American troops would shout vile things about the Japanese emperor, and in return the Japanese troops would chant the worst imaginable insults. Sometimes it would be "Fuck FDR!" Other times it would be "Fuck Babe Ruth!"

From the start of the war, there was reason to question whether America should cancel baseball, since manpower and materials were going to be in short supply. Not every American valued sport. Was it a luxury that a country at war could not afford? There was also the reasonable theory that the Japanese would take it as a sign of weakness if the U.S. were to call off the major league season.

Judge Landis wrote a highly diplomatic letter to the president on January 14, 1942: "Baseball is about to adopt schedules, sign players, make vast commitments, go to training camps. What do you want it to do? If you believe we ought to close down for the duration of the war, we are ready to do so immediately. If you feel we ought to continue, we would be delighted to do so. We await your order."

Two days later, Roosevelt responded with what would be called his "green light" letter: "I honestly feel that it would be best for the country to keep baseball going. There will be fewer people unemployed and everybody will work longer hours and harder than ever before. And that means that they ought to have a chance for recreation and for taking their minds off their work even more than before."

The president added that able-bodied players would have to serve in the military but that older players might continue to play, to provide employment for the players and entertainment, a sense of normalcy, for the American people. Bob Feller enlisted within days of the attack on Pearl Harbor on December 7, 1941, and Ted

Williams and Joe DiMaggio and hundreds of other players were soon in uniform, along with millions of more anonymous Americans.

Landis, not an admirer of President Roosevelt, kept his distance, knowing that Clark Griffith, the owner of the Washington team, occasionally dropped by the White House, reminding FDR that baseball was doing its part. FDR even allowed a few profitable night games, despite the frequent strategic blackouts and the energy shortage.

The major leagues decided to play a full schedule, despite crowded trains and lack of gasoline for cars and buses. In 1943, teams took spring training closer to home. The Dodgers trained in snow at Bear Mountain, north of New York, while other teams trained in dank armories, sometimes wielding bats like rifles as if somehow preparing for military combat. The White Sox gingerly forded swollen spring streams in French Lick in southern Indiana to get to a training field. The Cubs played in snow at the same site in 1944.

Night games were banned in most towns because of the fear of air raids. At other times, fans had to sit in darkened stadiums during sudden blackouts. Players were occasionally bumped from trains to make room for military personnel. Broadcasters and reporters were warned not to mention the weather conditions in their city, lest that information somehow get to the enemy.

By 1943, over 100 major league players were in uniform and over 1,400 minor-leaguers. A year later the figures were 500 and 5,000. Many of the best players were drafted or enlisted within the first year, while others were exempt because of physical shortcomings. Lou Boudreau, the player-manager of the Cleveland Indians, was classified 4-F because of bad ankles and led the league in hitting in 1944 with .327. There were some mutterings about exemptions like these, but many other men were also rejected from service for one reason or another.

"Baseball should have the right to use rejects if that would mean keeping the game going. Playing baseball is the most essential thing most of those fellows can do," said Albert (Happy) Chandler, a senator from Kentucky, who was fast establishing himself as a friend of baseball.

Among the old-timers willing to stumble back from retirement were Pepper Martin, Babe Herman, Jimmie Foxx, Lloyd Waner, and Paul Waner. Also donning major league uniforms were assorted policemen and sanitation workers, to say nothing of Eddie Basinski, a violinist with the Buffalo Philharmonic, who played for the Dodgers in 1944 and 1945.

Some Americans began talking openly about the injustice that blacks were dying for their country in service but were still shut out from organized baseball. "I can play in Mexico," Negro League pitcher Nate Moreland had been quoted as saying, "but I have to fight for America where I can't play."

Instead of hiring American blacks, the major leagues increased their recruiting in Latin America, looking for players who might not be pulled out by the draft. One of these wartime office temps was Preston Gomez from Cuba, who played eight games for Washington in 1944; twenty-five years later, in San Diego, Gomez would become the first Latino hired as a full-time major league manager.

Baseball had room for Joe Nuxhall, a schoolboy from Hamilton, Ohio—fifteen years, ten months, and eleven days old—who pitched two-thirds of an inning for the Reds in 1944, becoming the youngest player in modern baseball, and later a reliable pitcher and beloved broadcaster in Cincinnati.

The majors found room for Pete Gray, who had lost his right arm in a farm wagon accident at the age of six in the anthracite region of Pennsylvania. As a child, Gray learned how to hit one-handed, and he wore a tiny glove in the outfield, discarding it in order to throw. He played for Memphis in 1944 and was signed by the Browns in 1945, batting .218 in 234 at-bats.

Ballparks were utilized for war bond benefits and collections of clothing and scrap iron. Although many of their best young players went to service, the Cardinals won three straight pennants from 1942 through 1944, when they beat their crosstown rivals in the only World Series the Browns would ever see.

While the Grays and the Nuxhalls kept the sport going back home, many major-leaguers were directed toward service teams, both domestic and overseas. High officers competed for talent, and arranged cushy public relations posts for these stars between games, which were said to be good for morale. Wartime ball was no guarantee against combat. Murry Dickson, a pitcher with the Cardinals, was first sent to Fort Riley, Kansas, to join Harry Walker, Alpha Brazle, and Joe Garagiola of the Cardinals and Pete Reiser of the Dodgers, but that team was broken up and Dickson wound up on Omaha Beach in France on D-Day, June 6, 1944, and had a long fight just to get home.

Only two players with major league experience would die from combat: Elmer Gedeon, who had played five games for Washington, died in 1944 when his plane was shot down over France, and Harry O'Neill, who had played one game for the Philadelphia Athletics, was killed on Iwo Jima in 1945.

Some players were badly wounded, yet managed to struggle back into the majors. As the nation's most visible sport, baseball served up highly public examples of the human will to survive, to get back to normalcy. Bert Shepard, a minor league pitcher, had his P-38 Lightning fighter shot down over Germany on his thirty-fourth mission. He became a prisoner of war and his damaged right leg was amputated between the knee and the ankle. When he got home, he learned to walk with an artificial leg and trained with Washington. In July of 1945, Shepard pitched four innings against the Dodgers in an exhibition and then in August he pitched five and a third innings against the Red Sox in an official league game, giving up only one run. Shepard also visited the troops at the Walter Reed Hospital in Washington.

The war drastically damaged other careers, including that of shortstop Cecil Travis of Washington, who had finished second to Ted Williams for the 1941 batting title with a .359 average. Travis suffered severe frostbite in his feet at the Battle of the Bulge, and retired after the 1947 season. In later years, a baseball-loving lawyer in Atlanta, Abe J. Schear, campaigned to have Travis, a .314 hitter, named to the Hall of Fame as a "war hero," but to no avail.

Many major-leaguers returned with painful injuries and dark memories: Phil Marchildon, a Canadian pitcher for the A's, was shot down as a gunner over Denmark, parachuted 18,000 feet, was captured, and lost forty pounds; Earl Johnson, a left-hander with the Red Sox, earned a battlefield commission in the Battle of the Bulge and the Silver Star; Harry Walker, a future batting champion, later described to writer Richard Goldstein how he killed two German soldiers with a .45 revolver: "Your reaction was to live and that's about it"; and John Grodzicki took shrapnel in his right thigh five weeks before V-E Day, but pitched 19 games for the Cardinals after the war.

The players began to trickle back in 1945, even before the war was over. Hank Greenberg came back and hit a grand slam against the Browns on the final day to win the pennant over Washington. Everybody seemed relieved just to hold a World Series in 1945, with a mixture of stars and replacements, as the Tigers beat the Cubs, four games to three.

Memories of the war did not go away. Fans were reminded of the sacrifices every time Lou Brissie pitched for the Philadelphia A's. Hit by shrapnel in northern Italy late in 1944, Brissie underwent twenty-three operations, begging surgeons not to remove his left foot. He then fought his way back to the majors, wearing a catcher's shin guard to protect him from ground balls. In 1949, Brissie was chosen for the All-Star Game in Brooklyn.

On a personal note, my father took me to that game, pointing out the pitcher with the rather stiff gait. While we rooted for the National League, we also cheered for Brissie as he worked three innings for the other side. His career would last through the 1953 season, as he served as an enduring and visible surrogate for all the brave people who had suffered from the war.

———

Real baseball resumed in 1946, adding to the sense of hope. Having survived a war that threatened the nation's existence, Americans were eager to get back to family life and jobs and school—plus that familiar gathering place, the ballpark. To accommodate the players who had served in the military, major league rosters were expanded from twenty-five to thirty players. Ted Williams, after serving as an aviation instructor during the war, hit .342 as the Red Sox won the pennant. Stan Musial was back from the Navy, leading the league with .365 and helping the Cardinals beat the Dodgers in a playoff after the two teams had tied for first place.

To avoid growing rusty during the National League's playoff, the Red Sox arranged three exhibitions against teams of service veterans, including Joe DiMaggio, Cecil Travis, and Phil Marchildon. That idea backfired as Williams was hit by a pitch from Mickey Haefner and his left elbow swelled up. While Williams never used the injury as an excuse, he would hit only five singles in 25 at-bats in the Series. Musial would not do much better, with six hits in 27 at-bats.

The 1946 World Series, still regarded as one of the greatest in history, teetered back and forth into the eighth inning of the seventh game, when Harry (the Hat) Walker of the Cardinals, who had fought to survive during the war, plunked a hit into left-center, and Enos (Country) Slaughter raced all the way home from first base.

To this day, hard-core fans still debate the subtleties of Country Slaughter's mad dash with the same rapt attention that historians analyze the battles at Waterloo or Gettysburg. At first, the blame was attached to the Red Sox shortstop, Johnny Pesky, the relay man who allegedly froze with the ball during Slaughter's audacious run. At the time, Pesky accepted the blame, but over the years, as he became a venerable coach on his old team, Pesky recoiled from martyrdom, saying he may have cocked his arm once or twice but hardly "froze" before throwing.

Decades later, history has been updated to note that Leon Culberson, a reserve, had been pressed into center field when Dominic DiMaggio, the smooth smaller brother of Joe, damaged a knee in the top of the eighth. With DiMaggio on the bench, apparently trying to wave Culberson toward left field, Walker slapped the hit exactly where DiMaggio had feared.

The immediate message of the 1946 Series was more success for the Cardinals and more frustration for the Red Sox. But the broader message was that Ted Williams and Stan Musial were back.

———

The Japanese leagues did not resume in the first dreadful years of postwar rebuilding, but in 1949 Lefty O'Doul, a former major league batting star, brought his fabled minor league team, the San Francisco Seals, to Japan for an exhibition series.

"When I arrived it was terrible. The people were so depressed," O'Doul would say many years later, recalling how thousands of fans came out to see the Seals play, cheering "Banzai, O'Doul! Banzai!" in the surviving stadiums. Emperor Hirohito personally thanked the Seals at the Imperial Palace after the tour had raised over $100,000 for Japanese charities, but more important the visit led to the return of the Japanese leagues.

General Douglas MacArthur, who supervised the occupation, called O'Doul's mission "the greatest piece of diplomacy ever," a remark that remains an honored part of Japanese history. In January of 2006, while publicizing the first World Baseball Classic, to be held in March of that year, the Japanese ambassador to the United States, Ryozo Kato, would quote General MacArthur, recalling how baseball had helped heal the memories of war.

XII

JACKIE ROBINSON

He is an American icon now, his name perpetuated on an intimate parkway that twists through the hills and cemeteries of Brooklyn, the borough where he played. His number, 42, hangs in every major league stadium, permanently retired from use by future generations. Jackie Robinson is honored as the first black to play in organized baseball in the twentieth century, but he was more than a great man. He was also a great ballplayer, who could win games with his mind as well as his bat and glove.

It is virtually impossible to re-create the conditions of his debut in 1947—the long years without blacks in the major leagues, the taunts, the threats, the fear of failure. In 1947, in the United States of America, white members of the Philadelphia Phillies joined their Alabama-born manager, Ben Chapman, in shouting the most vile racial epithets at the twenty-eight-year-old rookie with the Brooklyn Dodgers, Jack Roosevelt Robinson.

"Hey, nigger, why don't you go back to the cotton field where you belong?"

"They're waiting for you in the jungles, black boy!"

"Hey, snowflake, which one of those white boys' wives are you dating tonight?"

No American has ever carried the weight of racial progress, plus his own career, as publicly as Jackie Robinson did. His daily batting average was one barometer of his success but so was the way he responded to barbs from the opposing dugout. He never faced attack dogs or fire hoses as demonstrators did in the civil rights era that followed him but he marched in his own way, the point man in a tense land. Every black politician, every black rap singer, every black athlete of today, every black citizen vaguely getting by, comes through Jackie Robinson, but without the incredible stress that wore Robinson down before his time.

Robinson was a hero who cut across many lines. Before Robinson, the most prominent black American athletes tended to be boxers, either "good" Negroes like Joe Louis (who did not voice his opinions) or "bad" Negroes like Jack Johnson (who dated white women). That was the standard. Then along came Jackie Robinson. I can still recall my father, who worked for a newspaper, calling from the office to tell us that our beloved Brooklyn Dodgers had brought up Robinson from the minor leagues for the start of the 1947 season. He became the soul of our team.

I consider myself fortunate that as a child and adult I would get to meet Jackie Robinson. Once, when I was around twelve, under the stands in funky little Ebbets Field, I was waiting to buy a hot dog when I noticed Robinson, who was injured and not playing that day, on line right behind me. I mumbled something about his injury, and he answered me civilly, patiently. I cannot resurrect every detail of that brief exchange but I do recall the blue satiny luster of his Dodger jacket, the gray of his hair, the bulk of his body. How could a man that large steal home so audaciously?

As a young reporter in the mid-1960s, I was working on an article about the status of blacks in sports. I called Robinson at home and asked to interview him, but instead he interviewed me, in his high-pitched, cranky voice: just exactly how many blacks worked in our sports department? "Um, none," I replied. His point, exactly. I remember that edgy conversation as fondly as I remember our brief chat on the hot dog line.

———

Jack Roosevelt Robinson was born in rural Georgia but grew up in the relatively integrated town of Pasadena, California. He played four sports at the University of California, Los Angeles, but was best known as a running back in football. While Robinson was in college in the early 1940s, black Americans were becoming visible in the military and defense industry, some expressing their resentment over the contrast with their traditional second-class way of life. Although Robinson had been a mediocre baseball player in college, his football exploits made him a candidate for wartime baseball.

After prolonged pressure from Lester Rodney, a reporter with the communist newspaper the *Daily Worker*, the White Sox were shamed into giving a tryout to Robinson on March 22, 1942. "Jackie is worth $50,000 of anybody's money. He stole everything but my infielders' gloves," the White Sox manager, Jimmy Dykes, was quoted as saying. However, Robinson was on his way into the service, and was not signed. After being commissioned an Army officer, he refused to go to the rear of a bus in Texas and was court-martialed, but was later cleared.

Around the country, there was pressure for baseball to open up to blacks. Mayor Fiorello La Guardia spoke out in favor of it. Joe Bostic, a black reporter, tried to force the Dodgers into signing black players. Leo Durocher, the abrasive manager of the Dodgers, volunteered that he had seen a number of blacks in Cuba whom he would eagerly manage, but Durocher's opinion was promptly slapped down by Judge Landis. The highly respected Wendell Smith of the *Courier,* a black newspaper based in Pittsburgh, lobbied Landis but claimed the response had been, "There is nothing further to discuss." According to Smith, Landis "died with those words on his lips."

Shortly after the death of Landis in 1944, the major leagues selected Senator Albert B. (Happy) Chandler of Kentucky as the new commissioner. Not known as a reformer while representing his border state, Chandler rose from his roots to set a tone for a nation in a new age. His finest moment as commissioner came almost immediately, as he promptly assured black journalists that the major leagues would soon be open to blacks.

"For twenty-four years, my predecessor did not let the black man play," Chandler recalled in 1982. "If you were black, you didn't qualify. It wasn't entirely his fault. It was what the club owners wanted. But I didn't think it was right for these fellows to fight at Okinawa and Iwo Jima, and then come home and not be allowed to play."

In that spirit, a Boston city councilman, Isadore Muchnick, pressured the Red Sox to take a look at Robinson, now trying to hold a regular position with the Kansas City Monarchs. On Monday, April 16, 1945, a couple of Sox officials put Robinson and two other black players through some perfunctory drills before excusing them. For the rest of his life, Robinson was so bitter about his brushoff in Boston that he would abruptly cut off any discussion of it. More than half a century later, the new Red Sox management, trying to exorcise its old ghosts, would apologize for the sham tryout.

Yet somebody else was watching out for Jackie Robinson: Branch Rickey, emboldened by the public proclamations of greater racial equality by the new president, Harry Truman, was seeking new talent for the Brooklyn Dodgers. There is a long and reasonable dialogue about whether Rickey was seeking to do the right thing or merely acquire better players for the Brooklyn organization, as he had done in St. Louis. Given the complexities of the man, it was probably both.

In all his years of stockpiling players, Rickey had never tried to hire a black player. As he often did, Rickey had a tale to go with his new actions: when he had coached at Ohio Wesleyan in 1904, the team had taken a road trip to South Bend, Indiana, where a hotel clerk attempted to bar a black player, Charles Thomas, from registering. As Rickey told it, he had insisted on sharing a room with Thomas, who cried and clawed at his own skin, wishing he could make his blackness go away.

Forty-two years later, the time apparently was right to make up for Charles Thomas's anguish. Rickey asked Clyde Sukeforth, a former major league catcher, and George Sisler, Rickey's first great discovery, to scout the Negro Leagues. He was looking for talent, but he was also looking for the right man to integrate baseball.

Rickey invited Robinson to Brooklyn under the subterfuge that he was starting a separate all-black Dodger team. Rickey tested Robinson, first in an abstract discussion about the confrontations Robinson could expect in the majors. "I'm looking for a ball player with guts enough not to fight back," Rickey said. Then Rickey turned up the heat, imitating the racist hotel clerks, railroad conductors, waiters, opponents, even teammates.

"Now he was a vengeful base runner, vindictive spikes flashing in the sun, sliding into Jack's black flesh," wrote Arnold Rampersad, a Robinson biographer. "'How do you like that, nigger boy?' At one point he swung his pudgy fist at Jack's head." Rickey did not desist until Robinson promised him he could endure any of that. He already had—in college, in the service, just by being black in America in the first half of the twentieth century.

When Robinson signed a 1946 contract with the Dodgers' farm team in Montreal, it was clear that Rickey was not recruiting him merely to fill out the minor league roster. Robinson and his bride, Rachel Isum, a nursing graduate of the University of California, felt comfortable in the French Canadian city, which did not have the overt racial edge of most of the United States. On the Royals, Robinson was tutored by an older teammate, Al Campanis from New York University, who taught him to play second base.

In the final days of spring training of 1947, the Dodgers promoted Robinson to the varsity. A few Dodgers planned a protest that quickly ended when the fiery Durocher informed them that Robinson was going to put money in their pockets. In early May, several Cardinals planned to boycott games with the Dodgers, but Ford Frick, the president of the National League, told them that anybody who struck would be permanently banned from the game. Frick said, "This is the United States of America and one citizen has as much right to play as another."

The Cardinals did not strike, but later in the season Robinson was spiked on the foot by Enos Slaughter, the star of the 1946 World Series, who was rumored to be among the players who talked of boycott. Robinson always maintained Slaughter had swerved to spike him intentionally, but Slaughter insisted Robinson had been injured because he had not mastered the footwork of a new position, first base.

Having promised Rickey he would not fight back, Robinson kept silent while bench jockeys like Chapman shouted vile things at him. Most of the Dodgers rallied around Robinson, particularly the captain and shortstop, Harold (Pee Wee) Reese, from Louisville, Kentucky. On the Dodgers' first trip to Cincinnati in 1947, fans began chanting racial epithets from the stands, upon which Reese put his arm around Robinson's shoulders, to demonstrate, in Reese's part of the world, that they were teammates and equals. Reese would later admit that his support of Robinson had not pleased some relatives and friends. (In 2005, a statue, suggested by Stan Isaacs of *Newsday*, would be unveiled outside a minor league stadium in Brooklyn, depicting Reese putting his arm around Robinson's shoulder.)

The Dodgers won the pennant in 1947 as Robinson, under intense pressure, batted .297 and was named Rookie of the Year. The next year Robinson moved to second base and became a much more productive hitter, with the guidance of George Sisler, who taught him to hit to right field. In 1949, Robinson led the league in hitting with .342. The numbers sound like the normal progress of a great athlete, but there was nothing easy about it.

On the road, he was fighting three battles at once. The game itself was tough enough, but Robinson also had to contend with threats as well as makeshift logistics. The Dodgers and the league office could not arrange for the first black players to stay in the team hotel in St. Louis, so Robinson had to stay at all-black hotels, which did not necessarily have air-conditioning or other amenities. The black neighborhoods treated him like a prince, but he watched his teammates head for the swanky hotel and he knew baseball was not sticking up for him. Every day was a battle. Then he had to go out and try to hit against Robin Roberts or Warren Spahn.

The Dodgers marveled that he did not break, although he and his wife feared he would suffer a nervous breakdown. After he survived his rookie season, the Dodgers began to catch a glimpse of the full Jackie Robinson, the college man, the battler, the officer who would not move to the back of the bus in Texas. After that first year of treading lightly, to keep his promise to Rickey, Robinson began to show his opinionated side, his anger, his gallows humor. One former teammate, George Shuba, observed Robinson up close in the intimate settings of the daily clubhouse. Years later, Shuba described how Robinson defused one tense moment:

"Visiting clubhouse, Cincinnati, 1948," Shuba wrote in a letter. "Jackie gets an obscene life-threatening letter. It states that he would be shot if he appears on the field that day. He posts it on the clubhouse bulletin board and laughs about it. If he didn't, he would end up in a straitjacket. We read it and are glad we're not him.

"[Gene] Hermanski reads it and turns to Jackie, who is getting suited up with the rest of us, and says, 'Jackie, I got it figured out. You haven't got anything to worry about. We'll all put Number 42 on our backs and that so-and-so won't know who to shoot.'

"Jackie says, 'Thanks, Gene, but I think that so-and-so will still be able to pick me out.'"

Robinson was followed quickly by other black players—Larry Doby signing with Bill Veeck in Cleveland later in 1947, the first black in the American League, Monte Irvin with the Giants, Satchel Paige with the Browns, Don Newcombe and Roy Campanella with the Dodgers, plus, briefly in 1949, the first dark-skinned Latino, Orestes (Minnie) Minoso. But Robinson had been the point man for all of them. He was a complicated man, who did not suffer foolishness around him, who could annoy his teammates with his high-pitched opinions. Newcombe, a superb pitcher and hitter, once told Robinson in the crowded clubhouse that he was "not only wrong, but loud wrong."

There was no escaping the tense reality that this social experiment depended on Jackie Robinson. If he cracked, or became unpopular, he could set back the cause of blacks in public life by years, even decades. Jack and Rachel Robinson felt the expectations not only from blacks—the invitations, the phone calls, the letters, the articles, the visits by celebrities—but also from whites who were rooting for him to set an example. The marvel is that with all this attention on him, Robinson became a great and versatile player on the best team in the league. He had been a mediocre shortstop in what was not even his best sport, but now, with the weight of the world on him, he willingly moved from first to second to third base and then to left field, depending on the Dodgers' defensive needs that season. He was already athletically middle-aged when he joined the Dodgers at the age of twenty-eight, yet he became a master of the crucial stolen base, the hard slide, the diving catch.

Perhaps the best game Robinson ever played was on the final day of the 1951 season, in the darkening gloom at Philadelphia. Having blown a lead of 13½ games to their rivals, the Giants, the Dodgers now had to beat the Phillies to force a playoff. In the 12th inning, Robinson dove to his left to snag a line drive by Eddie Waitkus. Tumbling and injuring his shoulder, he held on to the ball, to extend the game. Then in the 14th inning Robinson hit a home run to put the Dodgers into the playoff.

The Dodgers would lose that playoff in the third game on a three-run homer by Bobby Thomson, in what may have been the greatest major league game ever played, taking into consideration the rivalry, the squandered lead, the dramatic home run, and the presence of the acerbic dandy, Durocher, who was now the Giants' manager. Robinson is said to have been one of the few Dodgers who could bear to walk across the corridor at the Polo Grounds to congratulate their hated opponents.

In his decade with the Dodgers, Robinson helped win six pennants and one cathartic championship over the Yankees in 1955 that would justify that familiar October Brooklyn proclamation of "Wait Till Next Year." At the end of the 1956 season, the Dodgers traded the bulky, gray-haired Robinson to a team they had to know he would not join—the Giants. He thought about it for a few minutes and promptly retired.

At thirty-seven, Robinson needed to make money, but he also felt responsibility for other blacks. Despite a decade of watching dozens of blacks prove themselves on the field, baseball had no concept of seeking out minorities for jobs on the field or off.

Baseball was happy enough to discover the next wave of black and Hispanic superstars—Willie Mays in New York in 1951, Henry Aaron in Milwaukee in 1954, Roberto Clemente in Pittsburgh in 1955, Frank Robinson in Cincinnati in 1956. The Yankees, on the other hand, would not bring up their first black player, Elston Howard, until 1955, and the Red Sox, who had Jackie Robinson in their ballpark for a tryout in 1945 but couldn't wait to hustle him out the door, would be the sixteenth and last team to hire a black, Pumpsie Green in 1959.

The sluggishness of the Yankees and Red Sox would affect the balance between the two leagues. Up to Robinson's time, the American League had been clearly superior, but starting in 1947 the National League began to play a more aggressive and intelligent style of ball to go along with its obvious infusion of black talent. From 1933 through 1949, the American League had won 12 of the first 16 All-Star Games, but from 1950, the National League won 32 of the next 39. The only possible way to explain this superiority was that the National League was Jackie Robinson's league.

For all his contributions, Robinson was never offered a meaningful job in the sport, instead working in private industry to open up jobs for blacks and trying to convince his fellow Republicans to provide more opportunities in business. In 1962, Robinson became the first black to be inducted into the Baseball Hall of Fame, which he used as a forum to remind the owners that there were no black managers or front-office executives.

Suffering from diabetes, Robinson became nearly blind, having to be escorted onto the field when he made an occasional visit to the ballpark. His family and friends claimed the stress of his first years in the major leagues had weakened his system, as did the troubled adolescence of his first child, Jackie Jr., who came through drug treatment only to die in an auto accident in 1971.

Jack Roosevelt Robinson died on October 24, 1972, at the age of fifty-five. His name has been honored on schools and fields, as well as the Jackie Robinson Foundation, administered by Rachel Robinson, which prepares young people to work in the sports industry. The man who carried the aspirations of an entire race continues to open doors.

XIII

BASEBALL HITS
THE INTERSTATE

Whenever I visit Prospect Park in the borough of Brooklyn, my head jerks eastward like a compass, toward the apartment buildings where Ebbets Field once stood. In the tranquil Botanic Garden, I feel sick to my stomach, knowing that my team is long gone. I am not alone in this. I have compared notes with Fred Wilpon, the builder and owner of the Mets, who grew up in Brooklyn. The site of Ebbets Field is like the magnetic North Pole, constantly making us quiver in that direction. In the same way, Giant fans of a certain age feel visceral pain when they drive along the Harlem River Drive in Manhattan, past Coogan's Bluff, the hill that towered over the now vanished Polo Grounds.

Aging fans are the witnesses to the sudden departure of hallowed franchises in the first generation after World War Two. We suffered in the name of continental destiny. In the surge of prosperity after the war, people began to think about going somewhere. Families came back from their first vacation to Florida or California, raving about the weather, the new houses, the beaches, the date-nut shakes. In the frozen Midwest, people woke up on New Year's Day and turned on their brand-new television set to the Rose Bowl parade and football game from Pasadena, California, and pretty soon a family down the block packed up and moved out west. This happened every January.

America had been settled by pioneers twitching toward the west. In 1919, a young Army officer named Dwight D. Eisenhower had taken a two-month trip over rudimentary roads not much better than the rutted paths left by Lewis and Clark and the covered wagons. He never forgot the slow, torturous journey. In 1952, as the leading American general in the victory in Europe, Ike was elected president of the United States. One of his first priorities was to encourage two federal acts that would create over 41,000 miles of interstate highways, a system now named after him.

Baseball owners were not immune from thoughts of relocating.

In St. Louis, curly-haired, beer-drinking Bill Veeck began to entertain dreams of turning a profit with the Browns. As the son of the former owner of the Chicago Cubs, also named Bill, Veeck was a baseball man through and through, even if his fellow owners would never accept him because they found him too brash, too imaginative. Having had a leg amputated at the knee following service in the Pacific, Veeck tended to store his pipe ashes in the hollow of his artificial limb. That little routine would come off as amusing in a bar full of war vets or a pressroom full of reporters but was lost on the owners, as were most of Veeck's schemes and dreams. He would become one of the great showmen of postwar baseball, even if the other owners despised him and tried to break him.

After coming back from the service, Veeck had tried to buy the Phillies, until Judge Landis learned of his plan to hire black players. The owners preferred to steer the team to a man with a gambling problem, William Cox. Veeck then bought into the Cleveland team in 1946, touching off a golden age in that city. Veeck had this odd business belief that baseball was a very short step from a carnival: people would spend a few dollars on cotton candy and bright lights and a glimpse of the sword-swallower and the bearded lady. Baseball, in Veeck's humble opinion, was not exactly church—or even the opera. He provided daily gimmicks, including fireworks, giveaways, stunts, and games, setting a major league attendance record of 2.6 million fans in the world championship season of 1948. How that annoyed the other owners. Always short of money, Veeck sold the team in 1949 for twenty times what he had paid.

In 1951 Veeck bought the fading Browns, who had been beaten out by the Cardinals in what had obviously become a one-city baseball town. Once among the top ten cities in the United States, St. Louis could hear the population whooshing westward en route to California. To lure people into the ballpark, Veeck tried some new and outrageous stunts, including hiring a midget. Three-foot, seven-inch, sixty-five-pound Eddie Gaedel was promptly walked by the Tigers and taken out for a pinch-runner, but the league office nullified Gaedel's contract. In accordance with the old baseball cliché of "You can look it up," on page 916 of my edition of the *Baseball Encyclopedia* is the career record of Edward Carl Gaedel, born in Chicago in 1925, died in Chicago in 1961. (Bats Right, Throws Left, the *Encyclopedia* says, although Gaedel never got to show his stuff in the field or the base paths.)

The Gaedel stunt certified Veeck as a troublemaker, as totalitarian states come to brand members of the thinking class. The owners were not smart enough to heed Veeck's prediction that this newfangled medium, television, would soon widen the competitive gap between teams from the larger cities and the smaller ones. Most owners assumed they would keep making money at the turnstile, but peacetime attendance peaked at 20.9 million in 1948, Veeck's big year in Cleveland, and then began a downward spiral.

Losing money in St. Louis, Veeck reasoned that proud old Baltimore, still brooding since losing its major league franchise after 1902, would be an ideal site for his team. Since then, baseball had frozen in place for half a century, still concentrated in the northeast quadrant. At mid-century, California still seemed too far to move twenty-five players and their bats. The traditional overnight train rides from St. Louis to Boston in midsummer, with hot coal smoke blowing back into the Pullman cars (veterans below, rookies above), were long enough, without contemplating a road trip clear across the continent. The sturdy little two-engine airplanes that a few teams had begun to use for some trips were not capable of supporting a transcontinental schedule, over the Rockies. The Pacific Northwest seemed exotic; the Southwest was just emerging; and the Southeast was still getting over the Civil War.

Veeck's business logic was perfect but his fellow owners were committed to making him go broke right there in St. Louis, and they could make it stick, courtesy of the United States Supreme Court. In a nation that gave lip service to free enterprise, the industry was still protected by the 1922 decision that baseball was a game, not a business. The owners played a cutthroat game with Veeck, openly regulating interstate commerce by allowing only their friends to move.

When Milwaukee, still suffering from having lost its major league status after 1901, began making overtures for a team, Veeck might have moved there. Instead, the owners tipped off one of their good friends, Lou Perini, the construction operator, whose Boston Braves were losing money. In March of 1953, Perini was given hasty permission to beat Veeck to Milwaukee.

On opening day in early April, the Braves' damp, funky old park near the Charles River was vacant and desolate, and so were Braves fans, who could still remember Rabbit Maranville's artistry at shortstop in 1914 and had loved the pitching of Warren Spahn and Johnny Sain. ("Spahn and Sain and pray for rain" was the hopeful ditty of the Braves fan.)

Thus began a modern American phenomenon—the grumpy, aging fan who swears he has not been to a ball game since the Braves (Browns, A's, Dodgers, Giants, Senators, etc.) left town. But for every disgruntled fan back east, there were new fans in new corners of the United States, delighted to finally be labeled Major League. The reception was marvelous in Milwaukee, with the Braves leading the league in attendance five straight years from 1953 through 1957, going over 2 million the last four years. Ownership was able to develop young players, including Henry Aaron, and the Braves would win pennants in 1957 and 1958.

The owners proudly watched Veeck go broke in St. Louis, barely drawing a million fans in the three years from 1951 through 1953. The owners then magnanimously agreed to let the Browns move to Baltimore, so long as Veeck did not go with them. Baltimore, with its long and parochial memories, proved an excellent choice, just as Veeck had known it would. The Philadelphia A's, decimated by Connie Mack's fire sales and now under new ownership, moved to Kansas City in 1955 and promptly drew 1,393,054 fans in their first season, second only to the Yankees.

The profits from the three moves were not lost on Walter O'Malley, a lawyer who had gone to work for the Brooklyn Dodgers and gradually picked up some shares in the team, finally forcing Rickey out in 1950. The Dodgers led the league in attendance five times after the war and were solvent mainly because

O'Malley had been quick to negotiate income from television rights, but he could see himself making considerably more money somewhere else.

O'Malley soon pulled off one of the great real estate deals in the history of American sports. Insisting he wanted to replace dumpy but vibrant Ebbets Field with a new stadium in downtown Brooklyn or in Queens, O'Malley really had his eye on Los Angeles. First, he talked the Wrigley family, which owned the Cubs, into trading its minor league Los Angeles franchise to him. Then O'Malley charmed the mayor of Los Angeles into deeding him a ravine on the northern edge of downtown. Wild and crazy spendthrift that he was, O'Malley even promised to build a ballpark with his own money. He knew building a ballpark was a mere operating expense. Land was the main thing.

Next, O'Malley informed Horace Stoneham, the owner of the Giants, of this wonderful opportunity out west. The once proud Giants had slipped to New York's third team, partially because they played too many day games, mainly to give Stoneham more time at night to drink. The Dodgers and Giants, with their heritage going back into the 1880s, played their respective last home games before sullen, modest crowds in 1957.

In California, the Dodgers would play in the football stadium, the Coliseum, while awaiting their new ballpark in Chavez Ravine. Left-handed Duke Snider, remembering the snug right field at Ebbets Field, took one look at the miles of open space in right field in the lopsided Coliseum, and he quietly died inside.

The Giants played in Seals Stadium for two seasons while awaiting the building of their new ballpark, at Candlestick Point a few miles down the peninsula. City slickers from the East, the Giants owners had agreed to the new site, a bayside promontory, during an inspection visit on a warm and sunny high noon. They soon learned that every afternoon a savage gale screeched over the western hills, lashing Candlestick Point with full fury. The signature sound at 4:00 P.M. in Candlestick Park would be beer cans clattering down the concrete steps. Fans would bring blankets and down coats to night games, but were rarely warm.

With baseball finally on the West Coast, the two leagues still consisted of eight teams apiece, which meant the talent ratio was higher in the National League because of black stars like Mays, Aaron, Frank Robinson, Clemente, Bob Gibson, and Ernie Banks. Mickey Mantle, Al Kaline, and Brooks Robinson came along in this era, along with Sandy Koufax, a wild left-hander who came up with his hometown Brooklyn Dodgers, finally becoming the greatest pitcher of his generation, albeit in Los Angeles.

For better or worse, America was expanding—and so was baseball. Inevitably, the country was too large to permit baseball to remain at sixteen teams. Branch Rickey, the ancient sage, represented various cities eager to join the major leagues in a new entity, the Continental League. Rickey, who had prospered from baseball's exemption from antitrust legislation, now took the other side, lobbying Congress to repeal the 1922 Supreme Court decision that bound players to their clubs for life. Before Congress could pass any such legislation, the owners saw the wisdom of Rickey's argument and voted to expand in 1961.

The Griffith family was allowed to move its team from Washington to the Twin Cities, to be known as the Minnesota Twins, and two new teams were formed from an expansion draft—the new Washington Senators and the Los Angeles Angels. The American League owners were so inadvertently generous in exposing what they considered to be marginal talent in the 1961 expansion draft that National League owners vowed they would never let such a calamity happen to them. When two more teams were formed for 1962, the owners sheltered their best prospects on minor league rosters, leaving only culls and rejects to be drafted by the two new teams.

For the first three years, the Houston Colt .45s, named after the six-shooter that helped win the West, played in a rickety outdoor park, braving heat, humidity, and Texas-sized mosquitoes. I will always remember Richie Ashburn, a wise old outfielder with the New York Mets, demonstrating how he sloshed insect repellent all over him before a twi-night doubleheader in that malarial setting.

The theme park changed in 1965, with the team renamed the

Astros, in homage to Houston's space industry. Instead of exploring outer space, the Astros hunkered down under a roof, in the Astrodome, locally called the Eighth Wonder of the World. The builders had installed a grass field under a glass roof, but the glare from the sun blinded the players so badly that the roof had to be painted, as a result of which the grass promptly died. The faulty planning led to a series of green carpets for the playing surface, and ultimately to a product called AstroTurf, which produced erratic bounces and leg injuries, most notably the annoying phenomenon called "turf toe," from stubbing the toes on the ersatz lawn. Artificial turf, a downright blight on the game, would take more than a quarter of a century to eradicate.

Speaking of blight, the other expansion team was even worse than the one in Houston. The New York Mets—homage to a nineteenth-century team, the Metropolitans—felt the need to emphasize the glorious National League tradition. The front office accumulated old Brooklyn Dodgers plus other grizzled veterans, all of them past their prime, and for a manager hired Casey Stengel, who had won 10 pennants in 12 years with the Yankees.

This nostalgia exercise was responsible for the worst team in the history of baseball. The Mets lost 120 of 160 games but otherwise their first season was a joyous homecoming in the rusting, pigeon-befouled Polo Grounds. Stengel's rubbery face and caustic truths about his team ("We're a fraud") helped draw 1 million fans. From the start, the Mets captured a portion of New York fans away from the Yankees, who were merely winning their third consecutive pennant, plus the World Series.

All the old certainties were gone, including the old 154-game schedule that mandated four trips to every city. The new 162-game schedule became controversial in 1961, when Roger Maris of the Yankees hit 61 homers, thereby breaking Babe Ruth's record of 60. At first, Ford Frick, now the commissioner (and a former ghostwriter for Ruth), suggested that both records be recognized because of the unequal lengths of the seasons, but eventually all records were based on a full season, whether 154 or 162 games.

The major leagues continued to spread over the continent, with the Braves deserting Milwaukee, where the novelty had worn off, and moving in 1966 to Atlanta, which was just becoming a major American city. By 1998, there would be thirty major league franchises, including teams across the border in Toronto and Montreal, but only after a major challenge to the way the business was operated.

XIV

FREE AGENCY ARRIVES

I n the midnight hours, when Curt Flood could not unwind, he often painted portraits. His rendering of August A. Busch, Jr., his employer and the owner of the St. Louis Cardinals, hung in the Busch yacht, perhaps leading Flood to believe he was a member of some mythical Cardinal family.

By the mid-1960s, Flood was considered the best defensive center fielder in baseball, better even than the aging Willie Mays. He was also one of the many socially conscious African-American players in the most stimulating locker room in the major leagues in the 1960s, with vocal and intelligent players like Bill White, Bob Gibson, and Lou Brock. All but Gibson had been traded from their first teams and understood the cold business of their sport, yet perhaps three pennants had given them a false sense of security.

After the 1969 season, Flood was stunned when the Cardinals' management traded him to Philadelphia—nothing personal, just another of those trades that are said to improve both teams. Flood had played in St. Louis long enough to know he liked it there, and did not want to be shuffled anywhere without his approval.

Many other ballplayers over the years, whether white or black or Hispanic, had felt powerless when suddenly uprooted by a trade. Flood asked Commissioner Bowie Kuhn to cancel the trade but Kuhn refused. Given the owners' exemption from antitrust laws, Flood did not appear to have any options to void the trade, but in 1969 some Americans were not putting up with rules or traditions they considered unjust. They wanted to sit farther up in the bus.

Besides, Flood had resources that had not existed a generation or two earlier—a union, a real union. In 1966, the Major League Baseball Players Association had hired Marvin Miller, forty-eight, the chief economist and assistant to the president of the United Steelworkers, as the executive director. Used to dealing with hardened steel industry attorneys, Miller got the feeling the baseball owners had never quite met anybody like him.

"Essentially, it seemed to me, Miller had a deep hatred and suspicion of the American right and of American capitalism," Kuhn would write in 1987. "And what could be more the prototype of what he hated than professional baseball, with its rich, lordly owners and its players shackled by the reserve system."

There was another way to look at Miller: he was a labor leader, whose tactics and point of view were familiar to leaders in other industries. "To the owners, the union in 1966 was an aberration, a temporary irritation," Miller would write, years later. "Surely, they thought, once they applied pressure, the players would give up and I would be gone, and in a very short time. And who could blame them for such beliefs? They had ridden over every single challenge to their absolute authority and control for almost a century."

Miller recognized a more insidious problem: most baseball players accepted the owners' line that the reserve clause was needed to stabilize the business. This acceptance cut across educational and racial lines. Going back to the days of Albert Spalding and the forging of baseball as the American pastime, even players who came from a union background generally thought of union activity in baseball as vaguely unpatriotic. Like many Americans who buy the malarkey and vote against their own self-interest, the players tended to see themselves as samurai or cowboys, performing a noble act, in the American blend of open spaces, free enterprise, capitalism, patriotism. Their motto could have been: Don't fence me in.

Handicapped by the players' own ambivalence, Miller was trying to improve on the modest advances by earlier versions of unions. In 1946 a lawyer, Robert Murphy, helped found the American Baseball Guild, which forced the owners into providing pensions, a minimum salary of $5,000 a year, a maximum pay cut of 25 percent, and spring training expenses of $25 a week. Seven years later, the players, led by Ralph Kiner and Allie Reynolds, hired a New York labor lawyer, J. Norman Lewis, prying loose 60 percent of the broadcast revenues from the World Series and the All-Star Game for their pension fund. But in 1954, the players switched to Robert C. Cannon, a municipal judge in Milwaukee, whose salary was paid by the owners. By 1966, the minimum salary had grown exactly $1,000 in twenty years.

The owners had their scares over the years, particularly from the Pasquel brothers of Mexico, who in the mid-1940s raided the majors for a few dozen disgruntled players. Most players had scampered back to the majors when threatened with ostracism, but one New York Giant farmhand, Danny Gardella, claimed he was blacklisted and settled out of court in 1949, gaining $60,000. In a separate case, in 1953, a minor-leaguer, George Toolson, sued the Yankees, claiming he was being held illegally in their farm system, but the Supreme Court upheld its 1922 ruling that baseball was not subject to federal antitrust laws.

In February of 1968, Miller negotiated the first collective bargaining agreement in professional sports, raising the minimum salary from $6,000 to $10,000 and lowering the maximum salary cut from 25 percent to 20 percent. For all their success, the owners had reason to be nervous in 1970, noticing that the Supreme Court had studiously avoided giving the same leniency to football, boxing, or the motion picture industry.

For the first time in the history of the business, a star like Flood was willing to test the system. Thinking his clients were a generation or two behind the labor movement, Miller and the intense, artistic center fielder sized each other up. Miller warned Flood that the owners would try to destroy his career if he pursued legal action, but Flood insisted on going ahead. Flood then met with some of his peers, members of the board of the Players Association, whose main concern seemed to be that Flood was acting out of racial motivation. He had to assure them that he was seeking labor justice, although he would eventually compare himself to "slaves and pieces of property," shipped to another plantation with no say in the matter. Flood caught his peers' attention by giving up the Phillies' offer of a salary of $90,000 and vowing to sit out the 1970 season to pursue his case.

Flood lost one round in Federal District Court in New York but committed what was left of his money to an appeal. His family life was falling apart, and he fled to Copenhagen, Denmark, where he painted and waited for news from the lawyers. In 1971 he was offered $110,000, half of it up front, by Robert Short, the owner of the Washington Senators, who admired Flood as a player and a man. But Flood had nothing left. Batting .200 in his first 13 games, and no longer able to patrol center field, Flood bolted for Europe, keeping Short's advance money. For the rest of the 1970s he remained an exile, painting and playing guitar on the Spanish island of Majorca or in Copenhagen. He finished with a career batting average of .293 as well as seven consecutive Gold Gloves as the best defensive center fielder in his league.

His case moved upward. In 1972, represented by Arthur J. Goldberg, a former associate justice of the Supreme Court and United States ambassador to the United Nations, Flood reached the Supreme Court. The only players to speak on Flood's behalf were Hank Greenberg, a former owner; Frank Robinson, Flood's childhood friend and former teammate; and Jackie Robinson, visibly weakened from diabetes, months before his death. Many other players testified for the opposite view.

"I thought if the reserve clause went, baseball was going," Joe Garagiola, the broadcaster and organizer of a charity for indigent players, ruefully admitted many years later. "I was so wrong I can't begin to tell you. It took a lot of guts for him to do what he did."

In June of 1972, the Supreme Court, by a vote of five to three, with one abstention, upheld the lower court. Justice Harry A. Blackmun delivered the majority opinion that it was not necessary to overturn the "positive inaction" of Congress over the years.

The justices' reasoning seemed tortured and sentimental, as often happens when learned and powerful Americans confront sport, somehow assuming they should like it and endorse it, straining to seem like regular fellows. Perhaps the justices had bought into the old Spalding mythology of baseball as the backbone of America, and feared the country would stop functioning if players somehow had the same vocational mobility as electricians or schoolteachers. The justices seemed to sense the illogic of the 1922 decision; they just couldn't deal with it.

"I don't think I've ever read such criticism of a majority decision of the court by the very justices who formed the *majority*," wrote Miller, who seemed to have as much fun twitting the Supreme Court as he did the owners.

The dissenting opinion was delivered by Justice Thurgood Marshall: "Americans love baseball as they love all sports. Perhaps we become so enamored of athletics that we assume that they are foremost in the minds of legislators as well as fans. We must not forget, however, that there are only some 600 major league baseball players. Whatever muscle they might have been able to muster by combining forces with other athletes has been greatly impaired by the manner in which this Court has isolated them. It is this Court that has made them impotent, and this Court should correct its error."

With Flood living overseas, it seemed that he had lost his quixotic tilt at the national institution. The players had other weapons. In the spring of 1972, before the Flood decision, they had voted, 663–10, to go out on a strike that would last thirteen days and delayed the opening of the season. The issues were cost-of-living increases to health and pension plans. Miller also had what he considered a better and bigger plan for the next negotiations, having studied the Uniform Player Contract:

"The first time I read it, I did a double take," Miller would write. "What I had been told—and what the *players believed*—was that once a player signed his first contract, he no longer had control over his career. But the plain words of this section of the contract, as I read it, gave a club a one-year option on a player's services after his contract expired. *Nothing more.* It provided that if a club and player did not agree on a new contract to replace the one that had terminated, the club could renew the old contract for *one additional year.*"

The owners and their attorneys counted on the Flood case to maintain their hold on the players. They never saw change coming. In 1974, one of the best pitchers in the game, Jim (Catfish) Hunter of Oakland, believed his contract had been violated by the volatile owner, Charles O. Finley. Angry when he discovered he could not get a tax deduction for annual payments of $50,000 to Hunter's insurance policy, Finley had held back on the installments.

The case was handed to a professional arbitrator, Peter Seitz, who declared Hunter a free agent, setting up a huge migration of club officials to Hunter's home in rural North Carolina. On New Year's Eve of 1974, he signed a $3.5 million contract with the Yankees.

Hunter's defection was essentially a technicality, based on Finley's impulsive decision not to pay the insurance. A year later, Miller and the players had a more broad-ranging case: According to Miller's reading of the standard contract, Andy Messersmith had played out the option year on his contract with the Dodgers by not signing a contract, and was free to market himself to all clubs. Dave McNally, a former star pitcher who had retired, joined Messersmith in the legal action.

Once again, the owners allowed the case to get into arbitration with Peter Seitz, who ruled, on December 23, 1975, that Messersmith and McNally were free agents: "There is nothing in section 10 (a) which, explicitly, expresses agreement that the Players Contract can be renewed for any period beyond the first renewal year." The owners fired him as arbitrator "before the ink was dry," as Marvin Miller put it.

As a result of the Messersmith case, there was a lockout in the spring of 1976, followed by a contract that recognized free agency for players after five years of major league service. Messersmith, who had made $90,000 the previous season, promptly signed a three-year contract for $1.75 million with Atlanta in the spring of 1976, while McNally resumed his retirement. Baseball would never be the same.

The total major league payrolls would soar from $32 million in 1976 to $284 million a decade later. Seitz soon told reporters that the ruling could have been avoided had the "stubborn and stupid" owners attempted to negotiate. Years later, while professing personal admiration for the late Mr. Seitz, Bowie Kuhn would label the decision a "fundamental mistake," claiming that Seitz had displayed "a barely concealed anti-management bias."

Cable television money was in the air, and the players wanted to share it. In 1981, they staged a fifty-day strike over the owners' attempt to seek compensation for players lost to free agency. The owners settled when their strike insurance ran out.

Miller retired by the end of 1982, succeeded by Ken Moffett, a mediator familiar with the business, but Moffett was soon dismissed by the players. Miller came back for a while, followed by Donald Fehr, whose name was appropriately pronounced "Fear," a former legal counsel for the association. The average salary kept jumping from $51,000 in 1976 to $371,000 in 1985 and $489,000 in 1989 and $880,000 in 1991.

"I can remember that when I first came up, my goal was to make $100,000," Nolan Ryan, the great strikeout artist, said in 1979. "That was what I had always hoped for. Mickey Mantle made $100,000 and that was it. Nobody ever made above that. It's kind of hard to believe what has happened the past three years in baseball."

Gone were the days of walking unarmed into Branch Rickey's Cave of the Winds and being told, "Take it or leave it," however grammatically and scripturally correct. In the new money age, players sent in a proxy, a hired gunslinger, an 800-pound gorilla. An agent.

At first, general managers insisted they did not need to negotiate with agents, but, by the end of the 1980s, agents were formally accepted as part of the business. Among the best was Scott Boras, a former minor league player and medical litigation attorney, known for the elaborate books he prepares for negotiations, containing statistics and other arguments for the strengths of his clients. Some agents were better at personal hand-holding of their clients, others were better at negotiating contracts, but they became a powerful presence in the new money age.

None of this did Curt Flood any good. He returned from Europe at the end of the 1970s, broadcasting for Finley for a short time, but essentially out of money and energy. In 1982, Flood went to Cooperstown when Frank Robinson was inducted into the Hall of Fame. Robinson, the first black manager in the majors, paused in a gracious speech to acknowledge his friend:

"He was the first ballplayer who made sacrifices for free agency,"

Robinson said. "I don't think players today have given him the proper credit."

Flood had a hard final decade. He stopped drinking, but after years of smoking he came down with throat cancer. His medical bills of over $1 million were paid by the Baseball Assistance Team (BAT), a charity formed by former players like Garagiola and Ralph Branca.

In 1993, Flood was praised for having pushed baseball toward the age of free agency. "If that's my legacy, I'm proud to have been a part of it," he said. "It turned out to be not that bad: Attendance is better; television revenue is greater. I can't see where free agency has been so negative."

Curt Flood died on January 20, 1997, at the age of fifty-nine. The average major league salary that year was $1.3 million.

XV

WHY THE YANKEES EXIST

In 1996, the New York Yankees won their first pennant since 1981 and their first World Series since 1978. In the entitled world of Yankee fans, this is known as a very long time. The next day, a New York sportswriter took off on holiday, looking to get far away from the triumphal roar of Yankee Stadium. In the chilly courtyard outside the Uffizi Gallery in Florence, the sportswriter (me, that is) noticed not one but two Yankee caps, both worn by people speaking Italian. As they always do, the Italians looked fashionably chic and trendy, even in American ball caps.

This trend would continue at the next stop, London. Yankee caps, with that familiar logo of interlocking "N" and "Y," were ubiquitous, not just in the tourist sections but at working-class tube stops like West Ham, east of the city. Young people, sometimes of color, displayed the Yankee cap as a symbol of connection with the rest of the world.

The Yankee caps were sometimes an anachronistic green or red but mostly they were navy blue, the color of power, the color of success, the color of Ruth and Gehrig, DiMaggio and Mantle. All over the rapidly shrinking globe, Yankee caps caught up with the insignia of the fabled Red Ox of basketball (Michael Jordan's Chicago Bulls) as a sign of international sporting supremacy.

When the sportswriter got home to New York, he realized the Yankees were once again fulfilling the great polar needs of sport. Quite like America itself, the Yankees were either classic champions, envied and admired all over the world, or else they were haughty oppressors, resented by the downtrodden masses.

Yankee fans were relieved to find the moon and stars finally back in kilter, but Yankee-haters, in their own tortured way, felt relieved to finally be oppressed again in familiar fashion. As George Orwell put it, "If you want a vision of the future, imagine a boot stamping on a human face—forever."

Over the decades, the Yankees have managed to control or discourage just about every team in baseball, almost all the time. This had been going on ever since the two colonels, Ruppert and Huston, took advantage of Harry Frazee's need for money in early 1920, acquiring Babe Ruth for what seemed like a pittance even at the time.

The Yankees ruled the American League, winning six pennants in the 1920s, five in the 1930s, five in the 1940s, eight in the 1950s, five in the 1960s, three in the 1970s, and one in 1981. Then, after fourteen biblical lean years, they would win three more pennants in the 1990s and then three more at the very outset of the twenty-first century.

They did it with cold-blooded business sense, sheer skill, plodding callousness, outright panache, and what can only be described as Yankee luck. Jacob Ruppert's brewery acumen taught him to keep costs down and browbeat labor, and he hired a couple of cold-eyed men, first Ed Barrow, later George M. Weiss, to administer the financial thumbscrews. Lou Gehrig, the loyal captain, was perennially underpaid, but when Joe DiMaggio fought for more money early in his career, Barrow turned loose the yapping mastiffs of the sporting press to bloody DiMaggio's reputation.

Over the decades, the Yankees bought or traded for whatever they needed, but sometimes front-line players just fell into their laps. Tommy Henrich's contract with the Cleveland organization was voided, so he landed in the Yankee basket, and soon afterward became known as Old Reliable. Catfish Hunter, free from the erratic Charles O. Finley, chose to be a Yankee. There was always a new star who could be acquired.

Success begat success. The large population of greater New York engendered ticket sales that led to superior players—even superior managers, who had often learned their craft in the National League: Miller Huggins, the tiny, nervous former infielder with the Cardinals, won six pennants before dying young. Joe McCarthy, who impressed the Yanks from across the field during the 1932 World Series against the Cubs, came over to win eight pennants.

In 1949, the new ownership of Dan Topping, a wealthy scion, and Del Webb, a hotel and construction magnate, allowed Weiss to hire Charles Dillon (Casey) Stengel, the career National Leaguer who had hit a dashing inside-the-park homer in the 1923 World Series, temporarily upstaging Babe Ruth. Stengel had then managed in the National League, never with success, before going to the Pacific Coast League.

When Weiss hired him in 1949, Stengel had a reputation as a clown, a busher, a rubbery-faced mugger for the cameras, a mangler of the language. Very shortly, people figured out that the Old Perfesser was immensely smarter than that, that his syntax was an act. As cold-blooded as Ruppert or Barrow or Weiss, Stengel entertained the public at the same time he alternated old hands like Hank Bauer and Gene Woodling, right-handed and left-handed hitters, and made them accept it. He hastened the retirement of the imperious DiMaggio because he could see that the raw Mickey Mantle was going to be just fine in center field. And he won 10 pennants in 12 years.

Years later, in the age of George M. Steinbrenner, the Yankees would bring in Joe Torre, who had managed three teams in the National League with very modest results. Torre took talented players, restored calm to the clubhouse, and won six pennants in his first nine seasons. Think of it—30 of their 39 pennants were won by National Leaguers with no Yankee roots whatsoever.

The same magic potion worked with players. After the Philadelphia Athletics moved to Kansas City in 1955, Weiss organized a shuttle service with the new owner, Arnold Johnson, a Chicago real estate operator who had business ties to the Yankees' co-owner, Dan Topping.

Sometimes Weiss would salt players in Kansas City and recall them as needed. Roger Maris, a power hitter and superb outfielder, was summoned for the 1960 season and promptly won two Most Valuable Player awards, hitting 61 homers in 1961. According to one count, from 1953 to 1961 the cousins made eighteen deals, with the Yankees winning seven pennants and the A's never finishing higher than sixth. There was very little squawking from the fans in Kansas City, perhaps because their town had previously been a farm team of the Yankees, so all this coming and going of players seemed perfectly normal.

In some sad, subservient corner of the American soul, the Yankees were accepted as good for the game. Back in those days, the Yankees came to town four times a year, 11 home games per opponent, and they filled the seats. The Yankees made money for everybody in the so-called Brother-in-Law League, leading the league in attendance in 33 of 40 seasons from 1921 to 1960. Rival owners allowed the Yankees to buy or trade for the player who could give them a little pennant insurance. From Johnny Mize in 1949 to Pedro Ramos in 1964, there was always a vital spare part available for the Yankees. A few fans and reporters around the country protested these rather blatant shenanigans, but Congress had already shown its indifference to what would be considered antitrust violations in other industries.

From generation to generation, the Yankees won World Series in every imaginable fashion. They won with crushing home runs like Henrich's ninth-inning shot off Don Newcombe of the Dodgers in the first game of the 1949 World Series. Four decades later, Henrich returned to Yankee Stadium for an old-timers' celebration, and *Newsday* columnist Steve Jacobson lamented to Henrich that his tender schoolboy heart had been broken by that 1949 lightning bolt. Henrich, by now a septuagenarian, replied, "Tough!" And they both laughed.

Other crushing home runs were hit by players not known for their power, including Bucky Dent's three-run shot over the Fenway Park wall to help beat the Red Sox in the historic 1978 one-game playoff, and Aaron Boone's pennant-winning homer in the 11th inning of the 2003 seventh game of the League Championship Series.

The Yankees also won with magnificent defensive plays under pressure—Billy Martin's desperate lunge to catch a pop-up in the glare and wind of the 1952 World Series; Lou Piniella's sun-blinded stop of a base hit to slow down a potential Red Sox rally in that 1978 playoff game; and Paul O'Neill's lunge to snare Luis Polonia's screaming line drive, helping to turn around the 1996 World Series in Atlanta.

If Yankee prowess did not work, there was always Yankee luck. In 1941, Brooklyn seemed to have tied the World Series at two games each when Henrich (him again!) struck out, only to have the ball squirt away from the Dodgers' catcher, Mickey Owen. (Legend says that Hugh Casey's elusive pitch just might have been an illegal and slippery spitball.) Before you could say "Yankee luck," the Yanks won in five games.

In 2000, in the first Subway Series game between the two teams, the Mets made four base-running mistakes and the Yanks won that Series in five games.

Sometimes the Yankees were even perfect. In the 1956 World Series, Don Larsen, a playboy pitcher with the Yankees, somehow pitched a perfect game—no hits, no runs, no base runners whatsoever. (Yankee fans of a certain age still like to mess with the addled minds of aging Brooklyn fans by volunteering that the final called third strike on pinch-hitter Dale Mitchell was probably outside, but whatever.) Then in the Steinbrenner-Torre age, two gritty and complicated old hands, David Cone and David Wells, pitched perfect games on sunny regular-season Sunday afternoons in Yankee Stadium.

The Yankees dominated from generation to generation, watching other organizations ebb and flow: McGraw's haughty Giants, Mack's Athletics, the Cardinals with their vaunted farm system, the Red Sox of several generations, Cleveland in 1948 and 1954, the Go-Go Chicago White Sox of 1959. All had their hopes, but could not sustain them. For sheer torment, the Yankees did it most to Brooklyn—beating the Dodgers six times in seven World Series within 16 seasons. When Brooklyn finally won in 1955, fans rejoiced and said, "This Is Next Year," but as it turned out, it was the only year.

———

Finally, the empire faltered. On August 13, 1964, the Columbia Broadcasting System paid a relatively low price of $11.2 million for

80 percent of the Yankees. CBS assigned Michael Burke, a Cold War–era spy who had also run the circus, to guard the little fiefdom. One of the most charming and interesting people ever to run a sports franchise, Burke was out of weapons in this posting. Mantle was wearing down, Maris was injured and unhappy, and the farm system was empty. In September 1966, with the Yankees heading toward last place, CBS bought out Topping and Webb.

Under Burke's stewardship, Yogi Berra was sacked as manager after losing the 1964 World Series and Mel Allen was dropped as the team broadcaster. In 1966, after Red Barber alluded on the air to a dismal attendance of 413 fans for a September makeup game, Burke dismissed him, not one of the finer moments in Burke's otherwise splendid life.

On January 3, 1973, the Yankees were purchased by a group that included George M. Steinbrenner, the son of a Cleveland shipbuilder. At the press conference to announce the deal, Steinbrenner gauchely chortled over the low sale price of $10 million. Quickly pushing out Burke, Steinbrenner showed he was the boss—soon to be capitalized on the back pages of the tabloids as BOSS.

No detail was too small for Steinbrenner, who jotted down the uniform numbers of players he felt needed a haircut and badgered assistants to track down every windblown hot dog wrapper on the field. He bullied secretaries and fired assistants, although people learned to wait him out, since he was known to apologize with flowers or even a raise.

Steinbrenner was particularly tough on a series of general managers, banishing them to their hotel rooms to ponder a loss. He fired his field managers regularly, although he was known to bring them back, too, particularly the tortured Billy Martin, who won pennants, argued with the Boss, got into fistfights, and died in a car accident on Christmas Day of 1989.

Why was Steinbrenner like this? He sometimes explained that his father, the shipbuilder, had been extremely demanding, never satisfied with Steinbrenner's grades or his performance as a track and field hurdler. Steinbrenner apparently was going to take it out on his employees, one humiliation at a time.

Steinbrenner was also a creature of his time. The old Yankee owners had haughtily operated behind the scenes, with no need to appear in public, but New York in the mid-1970s encouraged more flamboyant magnates. A builder with eccentric orange hair and equally flaming ego, Donald Trump, openly boasted about his real estate prowess. An Australian-born newspaper magnate, Rupert Murdoch, set off a tabloid war with his formula of sniggering gossip. And Steinbrenner was not shy about playing to the back page of the tabloids.

The fans, apparently liberated of any inhibitions by the 1960s, were as demanding and mean as the owner, chanting "Boston sucks!" and other niceties. Yankee fans threw batteries at rival outfielders, jumped visiting fans who naively wore the logos of their favorite teams, and in general carried on like mini-Steinbrenners.

The Boss did spend money. It is unclear whether he anticipated the rising tide of cable television riches in New York or just lucked into it, but either way he spent fortunes on players, good and bad. Among his better investments were Jim Hunter, Reggie Jackson, and Dave Winfield, who helped win pennants in 1976, 1977, 1978, and 1981.

The Boss seemed to take his cue from having been born on the Fourth of July, surrounding the Yankees with patriotic rituals involving flags, anthems, military choruses, and, for playoff games, trained American eagles soaring around Yankee Stadium. The patriot also was convicted of making illegal campaign contributions, receiving no prison time and ultimately being pardoned by President Reagan. Later he was suspended from baseball for surreptitiously having paid a shady character for possible dirt on Winfield, with whom he had a feud.

Steinbrenner's suspension was the best thing that could have happened to the Yankees. He had stopped winning pennants after 1981 because of his addiction to buying expensive aging players from other teams. With Steinbrenner banned from running his ball club, executives like Gene Michael patiently nurtured an unprecedented crop of young talent—Derek Jeter, Mariano Rivera, Bernie Williams, Jorge Posada, and Andy Pettitte.

Reinstated, Steinbrenner let Arthur Richman, an independently wealthy and fearless old sportswriter turned éminence grise, talk him into hiring Joe Torre, a former player whose main assets seemed to be that he was a New Yorker—and a pal of Richman's. Once again, it was impossible to tell whether Steinbrenner was crafty or flat-out lucky, but under Torre the Yankees were back, cheered on by Mayor Rudolph Giuliani, who rooted from a seat alongside the Yankee dugout, with the city's modern anthem, "New York, New York," blaring nightly from the loudspeakers. Jeter, a mixture of the old-fashioned dignity of DiMaggio and the contemporary cool of a movie star, was named captain. In a new millennium, the Yankees filled the need for a glamorous and talented team to walk roughshod over baseball.

They expanded their horizons in 2003, signing Hideki Matsui, the leading slugger in Japan, who was known as Godzilla because of his powerful build. The first time Matsui put on the striped uniform he became a classic Yankee, perhaps not a DiMaggio or a Mantle but a terrific clutch hitter, a worthy successor to Henrich, Piniella, and O'Neill, the old reliables of their generations.

—

The rich got richer. After New York City renovated Yankee Stadium in 1974–75, the Yankees reached a season attendance of 2 million for the first time since 1950. But Steinbrenner was not satisfied, portraying the Bronx as dangerous, much the way Walter O'Malley had campaigned against downtown Brooklyn two decades earlier. The Boss threatened to move his team to either the West Side of Manhattan or New Jersey. Despite Steinbrenner's maligning of the Bronx, fans continued to pour in from affluent sections, reaching 3 million for seven straight years, setting a franchise record in 2005 with 4,090,692.

How much were the Yankees worth? On January 6, 2005, Richard Sandomir of the *New York Times* put together a few indications of vast income—the 3.77 million fans in 2004, the $64 million in cable fees from the YES Network, which the Yankees controlled, plus income from sponsors like Adidas. Balancing the income was a payroll of $187.9 million, the largest in baseball. Under new rules, designed to control owners' excess spending, Steinbrenner had to pay $63 million to the revenue-sharing fund and another $25 million in luxury tax payments.

"That meant," Sandomir wrote, "that $276 million went to players and less-wealthy teams, from total revenue estimated at $315 million to $350 million, before Manager Joe Torre, the coaches, the front office, the minor league system and the rent were paid."

In May of 2006, *Forbes* magazine estimated that the Yankees' value had reached $1.026 billion, the first American sports franchise to hit $1 billion. The magazine based its calculations on revenue of $354 million in 2005 and expenses of $77 million in revenue sharing and $34 million in luxury tax. *Forbes* also claimed that the Yankees showed a $50 million operating loss before interest, income taxes, depreciation, and amortization. However, Rob Manfred, baseball's executive vice president of labor relations, called the *Forbes* figures "not real in any sense of the word."

Any way you look at it, the Yankees' annual profit would seem to be in the millions, in a period when many teams insist they are losing money. The Yankees might even be more valuable, considering the future value of the YES Network.

Steinbrenner, who turned seventy-five on July 4, 2005, tended to stay closer to his home base in Tampa, Florida, behind layers of officials, publicists, bodyguards, and handlers. His two sons did not seem eager to take over the club, and he sometimes referred to his son-in-law, Stephen W. Swindal, as his heir apparent. The Yankee organization suffered from the impractical tilt of two poles of power, the Tampa faction and the Bronx faction, but nothing happened at Yankee Stadium that did not have the approval of the Boss.

Under his stewardship, the Yankees became ever more entrenched as the signature team of the United States—with touches of power, patriotism, quasi-religion, commercialism, dignity, and bad taste, often linked together in mind-boggling sequence.

For example: in the days after the attack of September 11, 2001, all baseball teams made the patriotic gesture of playing "God Bless America" during the traditional seventh-inning stretch. Years later, Steinbrenner was still observing this gesture, followed by a version of the secular baseball anthem "Take Me Out to the Ball Game," itself followed directly by the squawking video of what is apparently a drunken cowboy lurching to the jangled cadence of "Cotton-Eyed Joe."

Yankee Stadium has become a sacred place, like Westminster Abbey, with its memorials to ancient heroes tucked into Monument Park behind deepest center field. The dignified side of the stadium was permanently set by the nonagenarian public address announcer, Robert Leo Sheppard, a speech teacher and lay Roman Catholic lector, who delivered the lineups for a full half century. Sheppard's august tones were balanced immediately by the blatant cheesiness of mustard commercials, cartoon subway train races, electronic burps and tics, plus the vulgar chants of the Bleacher Bums.

Despite Steinbrenner's earlier campaign to discredit the Bronx, the Yankees seem destined to remain in that borough for a long time. A deal with New York City, announced in 2005, approved a new Yankee Stadium, just to the north of the old one, opening in 2009. The Yankees would pay for the stadium itself while the city would pay for the roads and parking. The new stadium would retain many familiar features and angles but would be placed behind walls, like a theme park—a totally American dichotomy of dignity and bad taste, something for everybody. Yankeeland.

XVI

THE WORLD CATCHES UP

I chiro arrived in America with a request. He wanted to be known, like a rock musician or Brazilian soccer star, by his first name only. He had left his family name, Suzuki, with his old team, the Orix Blue Wave. When he spoke at all, Ichiro spoke in brief riddles, almost like Buddhist koans, presenting himself to North America as a mystic from the Kabuki or Noh theater. He was also a control hitter, somewhat of a baseball throwback, not only to left-handed sluggers like George Sisler and Stan Musial but also to Wee Willie Keeler, a full century earlier.

How do you say "Hit 'em where they ain't" in Japanese?

He joined the Seattle Mariners in 2001, the first significant Japanese hitter ever to take his cuts in the so-called major leagues of North America. Sadaharu Oh never came. Shigeo Nakashima never came. But Ichiro came.

Slender and small, Ichiro arrived in a time of bulging muscles. Clearly, this was a man with nary a steroid in him. He trained on rice balls, bringing his own stash to the clubhouse, to the amusement of his burger-eating teammates. They did not smile patronizingly after he took his first swings, slashing the ball past infielders, racing to first base, stealing bases. In right field, he threw out runners like a latter-day Roberto Clemente.

By the turn of the new century, the game was thriving in two very disparate places, Asia and Latin America, not because of overt proselytizing like the Spalding barnstorming tours but because the game was fun to play. Ordinary people, often starting as students in America, had carried the game overseas with them. To baseball's credit, it had leaped the oceans, proved as attractive in Havana or Tokyo as it did in Boston or Chicago.

Baseball went first to Asia, starting in China in the international commercial city of Shanghai, where the Shanghai Baseball Club was formed around 1863. The sport arrived in Japan shortly afterward. The Japanese credit Horace Wilson, an American English professor at Kaisei Gakkô, now Tokyo University, with teaching the game between 1867 and 1873.

The first baseball game recorded in Japan was on September 30, 1871, between expatriates living in the international section of Yokohama and the crew of the U.S. battleship *Colorado*. In 1878, a railway engineer, Hiroshi Hiraoka, who had attended college in Boston and was said to be a Boston fan, organized the first Japanese team, the Shinbashi Athletic Club Athletics. As contact between the United States and Japan grew in the early twentieth century, the American leagues sent barnstorming teams. The A. J. Reach Co., rivals of Spalding, sent New York Giants and Chicago White Sox stars for nineteen games in 1908.

The game was quickly adopted by Japanese educators as an ideal and decidedly amateur outlet. By the 1920s, uniformed young men were playing for every school, with intense competition, leading up to the national high school tournament at Koshien, near Osaka, that is today the Japanese version of America's college basketball madness, the tournament leading up to the Final Four.

Professionalism came along when prominent companies saw sponsorship as a way to gain publicity. Matsutaro Shoriki, a newspaper publisher, had become friendly with Lefty O'Doul, the hitting star from San Francisco, who had toured Japan and fallen in love with the country. O'Doul urged Shoriki to form a professional team, which the publisher first named Dai Nippon Tokyo Yakyu Club—the Great Japan Tokyo Baseball Club. O'Doul, who was finishing up his major league career with the New York Giants, urged his friend to name his team the Tokyo Giants, and to adopt the orange and black colors of the Giants. Now called the Yomiuri Giants, after the vast publishing empire, the Giants play in a domed stadium in central Tokyo and have become the great national team of Japan, much like the New York Yankees in the United States.

In 1934, a group of Americans toured Japan, playing a memorable game in which Eji Sawamura, only nineteen years old, struck out four future Hall of Famers, Charlie Gehringer, Babe Ruth, Jimmie Foxx, and Lou Gehrig, in succession. Shoriki's Giants made a 110-game trip to the United States in 1935, with the help of

O'Doul, and the next year Shoriki organized a professional league, with O'Doul serving as his advisor. The Tokyo Giants even took spring training with the Seals before the 1936 season. O'Doul visited Japan every year until war broke out, and he returned in 1949 with his Seals, mourning the death of many of his old Japanese friends during the war, and inspiring Japan to begin a two-league baseball season starting in 1950.

—

As with everything else the Japanese adapted, baseball became a uniquely Japanese institution. Their greatest professionals lived in team dormitories (at least until they were married) and participated in repetitious drills almost year-round. A merry collegiate-style blend of noise and cheerleaders was encouraged at professional games but fans rarely booed players or managers. In a nation that prizes group solidarity, people considered it quite normal to have one dominant team, the Giants. The explanation was (and still is) that it is healthy for one team to be measured against all other teams. (Yankee fans would surely agree.)

The Giants attracted the greatest players, including Shigeo Nagashima, a powerful third baseman, who became the embodiment of Japanese charisma and talent. He was joined by Sadaharu Oh, the power hitter with a Chinese father and Japanese mother, whose name means "king" in Chinese and Japanese.

Oh's tale of failure and success is classically Japanese. As a child, he had tried to overcome the perceived flaw of being left-handed by batting right-handed. One day, a player in the highest Japanese league, Hiroshi Arakawa, was walking his dog near the local park and observed Oh batting right-handed but throwing left-handed. Arakawa told the youngster not to be afraid of being left-handed, advice that unlocked Oh's talent and led to his signing with the Giants, the highest possible honor for a teenage prospect.

As a rookie, Oh was given uniform No. 1, but his high-living habits in his late teens held him back. He was headstrong, resisting advice, the way he had refused to try the Stan Musial crouch when the Cardinals visited Japan in 1958. It was not until 1962, when Oh was failing, that Arakawa returned to his life. The Giant manager,

Tetsuharu Kawakami, knowing nothing about the earlier meeting between Oh and Arakawa, appointed Arakawa to be Oh's hitting mentor. This total coincidence would turn Oh's life around. Kind and caustic in turn, Arakawa ordered Oh to use the flamingo-style batting stance, raising his right foot, as part of his preparation to swing. This stance was adapted from a form of martial arts called Aikido, the Way of Spirit Harmony. Most mornings, Oh would work out with a wooden sword, learning to make such disciplined, powerful motions with his body that his sword would slice through paper. Then Oh would take the normal Japanese routine of work-outs and play in the Giant game that night. Arakawa's advice finally took hold, with Oh hitting 868 home runs in his career, leading the league in home runs 15 times, being named the Most Valuable Player nine times, leading the league in walks 18 straight seasons, and winning the Diamond Glove, as the best defensive first base-man, 9 times.

In the people's eyes, Nagashima was the soul of the Giants. "He and I were never really friends, though," Oh wrote in his autobiography. "We have never drunk together or had a social evening to-gether in the more than twenty years we have known each other."

"It wasn't so much Oh's Chinese blood as it was Nagashima's charisma and his 'seniority,'" explained Robert Whiting, an Ameri-can who has been a prominent Western observer in Japan.

One of the early Americans to play in Japan was Wally Yon-amine, a Hawaiian of Nisei ancestry, who arrived in 1951, not speaking a word of Japanese. Yonamine became a fine hitter and in 1974 managed the Chunichi Dragons to a rare pennant. In the late 1950s, the Japanese teams began bringing over foreigners, often for their power and potential at the gate. Japanese fans have fond mem-ories of George Altman, Clete Boyer, Willie Kirkland, Roy White, and the Lee brothers, Leon and Leron, who learned the customs and some of the language, but many other Americans took the money and did not try to fit in.

Some American players ran into the insularity of the Japanese culture. In 1985, Randy Bass, who had appeared in 130 major league games, approached Oh's record for home runs in a season but Japanese pitchers blatantly walked him, not allowing the foreigner to surpass Oh, himself not considered fully Japanese. This tactic was generally accepted by the Japanese people.

The first player to come to the American major leagues was Masanori Murakami, a twenty-year-old left-hander, who was assigned by the Nankai Hawks to the San Francisco Giants' system in 1964 as an experiment to see what he could learn from American teachers. Murakami did so well that the Giants promoted him from their Fresno farm team to the majors in September. He pitched effectively for the Giants in 1965 but the Hawks forced him to return after a legal battle in 1966. After a long career, Murakami became a broadcaster in Japan.

No other Japanese players crossed the Pacific for several decades, but then some established pitchers became restive with their highly restrictive contracts in Japan. In 1995, Hideo Nomo declared free agency and won 13, losing only 6, with the Dodgers, paving the way for other pitchers. After that, several of Japan's top hitters, including Ichiro Suzuki and Hideki Matsui, also came over, with great success, covered by a phalanx of Japanese reporters in every city in North America.

Through television, newspapers, and the Internet, Japanese fans became extremely knowledgeable about American baseball, investing some of their scant free time in news and games at odd hours from Seattle and New York and other American cities. Japanese players negotiated seven-year limits on their contracts and began to count the years until they could try their skills in North America. Some fans began to forsake their old teams, producing lower attendance and a few shifts of established franchises as well as labor unrest—all signs that baseball in Japan would never quite be the same.

That Japanese fans bought into American ways was evident in 2000 when the Chicago Cubs and New York Mets opened their regular season with a two-game series in the Tokyo Dome. The Mets' manager, Bobby Valentine, who had previously managed the Chiba Lotte Marines, was widely popular because he had learned to speak passable Japanese. In an official American game in Tokyo, with first base open, Valentine ordered his pitcher to intentionally walk Sammy Sosa, the Cubs' slugger. Normally, Japanese fans do not boo strategic moves by managers because that would violate the code of respect for authority, but the fans who had paid their way into the Tokyo Dome were hip enough to know that in the States a manager can be booed for avoiding a power hitter like Sosa. The fans let loose a chorus of boos, albeit with no malicious overtones. It was "American night" at the ballpark.

Valentine later returned to Chiba as manager, downplaying some of the accepted Japanese traditions like long drills before every game and having pitchers throw almost every day. In 2005 he brought along an American friend as promotions manager, his pal even bouncing around the ballpark in a mascot uniform to entertain the fans. Valentine's dashing ways led the Marines to a four-game sweep of the Japanese series. Having managed the Mets in the 2000 World Series, Valentine then called for a true "world series" between the North American and Japanese champions.

———

Latin America has developed its own style of baseball. While the Japanese leagues have existed for domestic consumption until recently, most players in the Caribbean region have had one major goal—to reach the majors and make money. Only Cuba, with its state-dominated league and tight controls on immigration, has kept its players at home, although defections by Cuban stars have been common.

Because of its proximity to South Florida, Cuba was the first major Latin outlet for baseball. Some say that Nemesio Guilló, a college student, brought the sport back from the United States in 1866, while others give credit to Esteban Bellán, who left the island to study at Fordham University in New York in 1869, became the first Latin major-leaguer with the Troy Haymakers, and returned to Cuba in 1874.

By 1878, there was a professional league, including Havana, Almendares, and Matanzas. Cuban sugarcane workers then carried the sport to the Dominican Republic and also the Yucatán peninsula of Mexico while American troops and oil workers taught the sport in other parts of Mexico. Venezuela's tie to baseball was established in 1895, but the sport really boomed after 1922, when oil was discovered in Lake Maracaibo, bringing the inevitable Americans. And Puerto Rico took up baseball following its independence from Spain in 1897.

Early in the twentieth century, Cuba was becoming a virtual colony of the United States, convenient for beaches and gambling and various other pleasures, only a few miles from the Florida coast. With a year-round baseball season, Cuba developed its own players and also offered a haven to black Americans who were banned from organized ball at home and therefore had considerable incentive to beat touring major-leaguers.

"I didn't come down here to let a lot of coffee-colored Cubans show me up," John J. McGraw is said to have grumbled after visiting with the Giants. Historians have counted 65 games between major-leaguers and Cuban teams, with a direct split of 32-32-1. Jose Mendez, one of Cuba's greatest pitchers, won eight of those games.

In the early twentieth century, many Latinos hoped to play in the major leagues but never got the chance because of America's national obsession about race. Martin Dihigo, a Cuban who led the Mexican League in batting in 1938 with a .387 average and also won 18 games as a pitcher with an earned run average of 0.90, was too dark-skinned for the majors, although he would eventually be voted into the Hall of Fame.

Some players did slip under the American visual skin-tone barrier. Clark Griffith, while operating the Cincinnati Reds, hired Rafael Almeida and his translator, Armando Marsans, whose complexion was called "olive-skinned," and later when Griffith moved to Washington he signed light-skinned Latinos at modest salaries.

One Cuban who passed the visual barrier was Miguel Gonzalez, a catcher who became the first Latino manager, filling in for 17 games with the Cardinals late in the 1938 season. Gonzalez was also the third-base coach when Enos Slaughter steamed home with the winning run in the 1946 World Series, and Gonzalez was later the scout who coined the immortal evaluation: "good field, no hit."

The first big star from Latin America was Adolfo Luque, a

pitcher born in 1890 in Cuba. After bouncing around, Luque joined Cincinnati in 1918 and bloomed under his manager, Christy Mathewson. Luque pitched the first shutout by a Latino, and in 1919 became the first Latino to play in the World Series. Although he often heard heckling about his swarthy skin, Luque had the aggressive temperament to give it right back, lasting long enough to save the 1933 World Series for the Giants.

Luque is a classic example of the six-degree connections in baseball. After World War Two, during the Pasquel brothers' expensive raids on the majors, Luque was managing the Puebla team in Mexico. One of his pitchers was Sal Maglie, a refugee from the Giants, who had previously pitched for Luque in winter ball in Cienfuegos, Cuba.

Years later, Maglie would tell how Luque lectured him to throw a curveball—"like Mardy."

"Mardy? Who's that?" Maglie had asked.

"Mardy! Mardy! You never heard of Chreesty Mardyson?" Luque replied in his chewy Cuban accent.

After Luque's tutelage, Maglie returned to the States as a hard-bitten old pro, mostly with the Giants, later with Brooklyn. In 1956, Maglie was a teammate of a lanky rookie named Don Drysdale, imparting his wisdom about when and how to pitch inside, which Drysdale adapted with great relish. Thus, there is a direct baseball lineage from Mathewson, the Hall of Famer early in the century, through Luque and Maglie, to Drysdale, an eventual Hall of Famer.

The ethnic barriers fell slightly, out of necessity, during World War Two. Some teams, particularly Washington, signed Latin players who happened to be light-skinned and were not about to be drafted for the military. Needing reasonably able-bodied players, Griffith and other owners were less likely to inspect the color of their imports from Cuba.

Two years after the arrival of Jackie Robinson and other pioneers in 1947, Cleveland brought in Orestes Arrieta Armas, who went by his stepbrothers' family name of Minoso. Nicknamed "Minnie," he was promptly traded to the White Sox, where he became Rookie of the Year and was soon considered a Chicago civic treasure up to his retirement in 1964. Minoso made cameo appearances in the 1970s and 1980s but was stopped from playing in another decade in 1990 when Commissioner Fay Vincent refused to permit any such Veeckian-style tomfoolery.

Roberto Clemente from Carolina, Puerto Rico, became the first Latino superstar. He signed with the Dodgers for a bonus of $10,000, but under the rules of the day Clemente either had to play for the parent team in Brooklyn or be eligible for a draft by another system. The Dodgers tried to hide him at their Montreal farm team in 1954, but the rumpled veteran Pittsburgh scout Howie Haak noticed Clemente on his rare appearances and quickly recommended him to the Pirates' general manager—none other than Branch Rickey. Rickey, who had been forced out by Walter O'Malley, delightedly drafted Clemente, and turned him over to mentors, including—the reader has already guessed—George Sisler.

Sisler showed Clemente how to make tighter turns while running the bases, and how to keep his head from bobbing at the plate. Clemente broke in with the Pirates in 1955, helped them win the World Series in 1960, and won the batting championship in 1961 with a .351 average. Later he thanked the Pirates coaches, including Sisler, for their encouragement.

Proud, intelligent, handsome, and outspoken on the subject of race—plus a graceful right fielder with a superb arm and quick bat—Clemente became a superstar. In the last days of 1972, following an earthquake in Nicaragua, Clemente chartered a plane in Puerto Rico, loaded it himself with relief supplies, and prepared to fly there, but the plane crashed into the sea upon takeoff. He quickly became one of the few players ever inducted into the Hall of Fame before the mandatory five-year waiting period. To this day, many Latino players wear No. 21 in his honor.

After Minoso and Clemente arrived, it was obvious that Latin America was a gold mine for talent. The Giants found the three Alou brothers in the Dominican Republic, along with Juan Marichal. After the Dodgers discovered Fernando Valenzuela in Mexico, their 1981 attendance was an average of 9,000 higher on the days of his scheduled starts at home.

No country in the world loves baseball more than Cuba, both before and after the 1959 revolution. Fidel Castro has never discouraged the myth that he was once a hot pitching prospect, but in reality his highest level was pitching for his decidedly amateur law school team. Under Castro, the state-supported national team has dominated world amateur tournaments, but Castro has refused to allow his players to earn a salary in professional leagues outside the country. Many Cuban stars found a way to leave, starting with young Tony Perez and Tony Oliva after the revolution and followed, years later, by Orlando (El Duque) Hernandez, who slipped out by sea, either on a leaky raft or a high-powered yacht, depending on who is doing the telling. In 1998, somewhere in his thirties, El Duque established himself as a fearless winner of big games for the Yankees. Nicaragua also closed its borders for a time, but Dennis Martinez managed to sign with Baltimore in 1973 and had a long and successful career in the major leagues.

Many major league teams, recognizing the talent pool in Latin America, began establishing academies, particularly in the Dominican Republic. In 2005, the Mets brought over Omar Minaya as their general manager after he had helped keep the shaky Montreal Expos competitive.

Minaya, of Dominican ancestry and raised in Queens, a few blocks from Shea Stadium, was given a large budget for restocking the Mets. He promptly signed Pedro Martinez, the ace Dominican pitcher, as well as Carlos Beltran and later Carlos Delgado, two Puerto Rican sluggers, who served as walking advertisements that the Mets were receptive to talent, wherever its origins.

———

Meanwhile, Ichiro (or "Suzuki," as he is still listed in baseball's finicky computer system) established himself as one of the great hitters in the major leagues, making 242, 208, and 212 hits in his first three seasons.

In 2004, he began to challenge the record for hits in a single season, 257, set back in 1920 by George Sisler. In America, fans were inflamed by home runs but Japan was captivated by Ichiro's chase of Sisler, who had died in 1973. When it became obvious that Ichiro might break the record, members of Sisler's family were invited to Seattle on the final weekend of the season.

"If my grandfather were here today, he would say of Ichiro that he is a professional baseball player and would not want to talk about where he was from," said William Drochelman, meaning that his grandfather would not care about the race of the player who broke his record.

After slapping a single up the middle, breaking the record that had lasted eighty-four years, Ichiro jogged toward the stands, waving his batting helmet for Sisler's daughter, Frances Drochelman of St. Louis, eighty-one years old. He did not perform a deep ceremonial bow as he might have done in Japan, but he smiled at Sisler's daughter, who applauded, shook his hand, and patted him on the shoulder.

"There was so little time, and with the language barrier, I just thanked them for coming," Ichiro told reporters later.

Ichiro's opponents, the Texas Rangers, got into the spirit. The four infielders lined up near second base, removed their caps, and bowed deeply.

———

By the twenty-first century, fully a quarter of all major-leaguers came from abroad. By contrast, the number of African-Americans in the major leagues had fallen to 9 percent by 2005. The sport of Jackie Robinson and Willie Mays was now perceived as a "white man's sport" by many black Americans, who tended to play football and basketball. Black fans, who had flocked to the integrated major leagues after World War Two, were now a distinct minority in the modern stadiums of America. By 2006, Major League Baseball was encouraging urban baseball academies in the United States to match the twenty academies that trained the eager talent in the Dominican Republic.

The sport continued to grow around the world after being officially added to the Olympic schedule in Seoul in 1988. Countries like China and Russia recruited athletes from other sports to learn baseball's specialized techniques. Unfortunately, Major League Baseball did not allow its players to take time off for the Olympic tournament every four years because it inevitably fell during the regular season. Perhaps Major League Baseball was hesitant to expose its players to the rigid Olympic testing for performance-enhancing drugs. The International Olympic Committee, seeking to streamline the Summer Games, voted to drop baseball after the 2008 Summer Games in Beijing.

Needing to find its own path to a world forum, Major League Baseball organized a sixteen-nation tournament in March 2006, trying to emulate the World Cup of soccer, the most popular sports event on earth. The new World Baseball Classic included stars like Derek Jeter from the United States; David Ortiz from the Dominican Republic; Mike Piazza representing Italy, the nation of his grandparents; and Ichiro Suzuki from Japan. South Korea beat the United States out of a place in the semifinals and Cuba stunned Puerto Rico in San Juan for a place in the semifinals. The proud and edgy Cubans, wearing bright red uniforms—with Fidel's son Antonio serving as team doctor, counselor, and cheery commissar in the dugout—advanced to the finals against Japan.

In the championship game in San Diego, the Japanese prevailed over the Cubans, 10–6. Many Americans grumbled that holding the tournament in March, during the early days of spring training, did not allow the Americans to play at their best, but the reality was that the Japanese and Cubans and South Koreans all outworked the United States with sound fundamentals and desire. The absence of the American squad in the finals was a huge boost to the credibility of the tournament and an advertisement for the growth of baseball around the world. The organizers hoped to work out some of the flaws by the next Classic in 2009, but a World Cup–style tournament seems to be the way for baseball to continue growing around the world.

XVII

SAME GAME, YUPPIFIED

If Alexander Cartwright or Doc Adams were ushered into a modern ballpark, he would surely recognize the sport itself, right down to the strutting athletes who hit and run, spit and scratch, just like the old-timers. But the ancient builders of the sport might be mystified by the dreadful din blasting from the loudspeakers or the air-conditioned luxury boxes separating the shrimp-eaters and wine-drinkers from the actual fans. ("Sushi? What is this sushi?" Cartwright or Adams might well ask.)

They would also demand a careful explanation of some strange doings on the field. Are those gigantic gloves really necessary? What is all that equipment on the catcher? And who is this interloper who comes out to bat every few innings and then disappears without ever playing in the field?

Baseball has continued to evolve, every day, every season, sometimes generically and sometimes artificially, often accompanied by loud and long debate. Many of the changes divide fans into conservatives and liberals. Every innovation produces purists and high priests who believe the game should never be monkeyed with, and more tolerant souls who ask, "What's the big deal?"

No change has divided people more openly than the designated hitter rule, which was installed in 1973 in the American League, and where it festers still. The DH, as it is called, authorizes a hitter to bat in place of the pitcher, who has almost always been the weakest batter in any lineup. The rule was designed to make American League lineups more potent from top to bottom, to appeal to fans who like to see runners crossing the plate and are less charmed by good pitching and good defense.

The rule has also guaranteed that the two major leagues play different versions of the game. National League teams stock up on specialists who can pinch-hit, pinch-run, or play defense in the late innings while the American League tends to send out nine sluggers and let them swing away. Trying to be fair and neutral about it, I can only say that the designated hitter rule is a travesty, and ought to be tossed out.

Here are more than 125 years of innovations, major and minor:

1876: A Harvard student, Fred Thayer, adapted a fencing mask for Alexander Tyng, a catcher with the Harvard team. (Earlier, Harry Wright of the Cincinnati Red Stockings had devised a rubber mouthguard to protect the catcher's teeth, but a mask was at first decried as not exactly masculine.)

1876: Albert G. Spalding designated caps of different colors to every field position. His White Stockings were described by a sportswriter as "a Dutch bed of tulips."

1882: Brother Jasper of Manhattan College urged fans to stand up and cheer in the bottom half of the seventh inning, before the home team's turn at bat. The "seventh-inning stretch" soon spread to the majors, where it is today embellished with versions of "Take Me Out to the Ball Game," blasted over modern sound systems and animated message boards.

1885: Art Irwin of Providence used the first fielder's glove, cutting holes in the fingertips of work gloves to allow fielders to get a grip.

1888: The Washington Capitols were the first team to take spring training in the Deep South, spending three weeks in Florida. "When we arrived in Jacksonville," recalled Connie Mack, a young catcher on that team, "four of our 14 players were reasonably sober. The rest were totally drunk. There was a fight every night, and the boys broke up a lot of furniture. We played exhibition games by day and drank much of the night."

By the turn of the century, John McGraw took his Giants to end-of-the-world Texas and made them trudge a mile or two from their rustic hotel to their dusty training site, as if to clean out the toxins of the winter by sheer torture. Later in the twentieth century, Florida and Arizona grew more hospitable, and so did spring training.

1889: Four balls constituted a walk, after counting as a hit for many years.

1890s: The Brooklyn Bridegrooms invented the cutoff play, in which infielders lined up to handle throws from the outfield. In an ironic turn of events, their descendants, the Dodgers of the 1920s, would be known for their clumsiness and poor tactics, once having three runners wind up on third base.

1901: The National League made the first two fouls count as strikes, a new advantage for the pitcher.

1907: The Giants' catcher, Roger Bresnahan, wore fiber shin guards over his pants, much as cricket players did. Previously, catchers had stuffed newspapers under their slacks to protect against the ball, as visible shin guards were first seen as a character flaw.

1907: Later that season, Bresnahan was hit by a pitch and after a month in the hospital he returned, wearing a rudimentary inflatable batting helmet designed by Frank Pierce Mogridge. In baseball's slow fashion, batting helmets would be resisted, even after Cleveland shortstop Ray Chapman was killed by a pitch from Carl Mays of the Yankees in 1920. In the early 1920s, some players would experiment with leather headgear similar to football helmets, but they were met with sarcasm from other players.

1908: A tarpaulin was introduced in Pittsburgh, to protect the field during rain.

1910: President William Howard Taft became the first president to throw out a ball on opening day.

1920: Batters were credited with a sacrifice fly (and no at-bat) when a runner scored from third on a fly ball.

1922: Bill Doak, a pitcher with Branch Rickey's Cardinals, sewed a leather strip between the thumb and index finger on his glove, thereby creating the earliest pocket.

1925: The first player known to use a personal trainer was none other than Babe Ruth, who lost forty-one pounds over the winter.

1929: The Yankees were the first team to use a pitching coach, Bob Shawkey. By the turn of the century, teams would have a pitching coach in the dugout and another in the bullpen.

1929: The first amplifier in a ballpark was at the Polo Grounds. So now you know whom to blame for the earsplitting racket in ballparks today.

1929: Picking up on a brief experiment by Cleveland in 1916, the Yankees began wearing uniform numbers on their backs, based on the regular batting order: Earle Combs No. 1, Mark Koenig No. 2, Babe Ruth No. 3, Lou Gehrig No. 4, Bob Meusel No. 5, Tony Lazzeri No. 6, Leo Durocher No. 7. With three catchers, Johnny Grabowski was No. 8, Benny Bengough No. 9, and Bill Dickey No. 10, although Dickey later switched to No. 8.

1938: The Dodgers experimented with yellow baseballs, which theoretically made them easier to see, but the idea was dropped. This idea would be revived in the mid-1960s by Charles O. Finley of Kansas City, who preferred orange balls, but was never adapted, perhaps because it had been proposed by the cantankerous Mr. Finley.

1941: After Pee Wee Reese and Joe Medwick were hit by pitches in 1940, the Brooklyn owner, Larry MacPhail, with advice from doctors, created solid inserts for ball caps.

1952: The new Pittsburgh president, Branch Rickey, had plastic batting helmets built by the American Baseball Cap Company (which he happened to own). Players complained but both leagues made helmets mandatory later in the decade.

1953: Comme père, comme fils: Bill Veeck revived his father's talk of interleague play, but the owners turned it down, probably because of its source.

1954: Players were no longer allowed to leave their gloves on the lip of the outfield grass between innings, as had been the custom. Gloves were still relatively crude and stubby, but modern technology began to produce large, supple gloves with deep pockets.

1965: Indoor baseball began at the Astrodome in Houston, leading to the blight of artificial turf.

1970s: In the decade of disco, A. G. Spalding's animated tulips got a reprieve with some of the most ghastly uniforms ever seen: the brown-orange-and-yellow uniform of the San Diego Padres (Steve Garvey said he felt like a taco); the space-age disaster of red, yellow, and orange of the Houston Astros; Oakland's kelly green and gold uniforms (which dated back to 1963), with white shoes that made them look like cartoon characters; Cleveland's all-red uniforms and Pittsburgh's all-yellow outfits. In 1976, navy-blue Bermuda shorts and white nylon pullovers were briefly foisted upon the White Sox, but heckled into history after three games. (At least owner Bill Veeck had an excuse: the shorts had been designed by his wife, Mary Frances.)

1973: The American League's first designated hitter, Ron Blomberg of the Yankees, asked the wise old coach, Elston Howard, how to approach his new role. "Go hit and then sit down," Howard instructed. (For the record, Blomberg drew a bases-loaded walk.) Since then, the DH has kept older, slower stars like Edgar Martinez, Harold Baines, Hal McRae, Tommy Davis, and Paul Molitor in the game at relatively high salaries.

As a result of the DH, the American League is known for more runs and longer games while the National League is known for more interesting strategy along with the occasional pitcher who can help himself via hitting and base running. Then there is the annual botch-up in the World Series that began with the rule being used in alternating years, but now has all Series games played under the rules of the home team, meaning that both teams are disrupted from their normal strategy.

1995: The wild card. After a brutal labor dispute canceled the 1994 World Series, the playoffs were enlarged to a three-tiered system, with three division winners and the wild-card team with the fourth-best record in each league. At first it sounded like another crass gimmick, but a superb first round between Seattle and the Yanks guaranteed that the wild card was here to stay, despite evidence of wear and tear on the best pitchers' arms.

1997: Catcher Charlie O'Brien of Toronto began using a helmet merged into the now traditional mask, making him look halfway between a hockey goalie and a football player. The invention was soon adapted by many catchers to avoid concussions from the batter's backlash and foul tips. Two decades earlier, Bill Buhler, the trainer of the Dodgers, had invented a throat guard that hung down from the catcher's mask, after Steve Yeager had been seriously injured when a splintered bat hit him in the throat. The guard was said to resemble a goat's beard.

1997: Interleague play arrived, with heavy emphasis on regional rivalries like Yankees-Mets, Dodgers-Angels, Cubs–White Sox. The midseason gimmick also produced a glut of uninteresting matchups between teams with no connections, but officials finally introduced a more equitable round-robin schedule, so that popular teams like the Yankees and Red Sox would ultimately visit every National League park.

Along with changes in equipment and rules, teams also came up with more refined management procedures and strategies. By the twenty-first century, instead of having a drinking buddy or two tag along as coaches, managers were allowed five coaches in uniform during games, including a so-called bench coach, a sort of manager's manager. In addition, teams had medical staffs, trainers, nutritionists, weight experts, physical therapists, and psychologists. Latter-day sluggers demanded their personal trainers have entrée to the clubhouse, although this practice was slowed down in the wake of the steroid scandals.

Some of the biggest changes in the game involved pitching, evolving from the age of iron men like Jack Chesbro and Iron Joe McGinnity, who almost always finished their games. By the twenty-first century, starting pitchers were proudly called "inning-eaters" if they could last five or six innings without major damage, and they were practically nominated for the Hall of Fame if they staggered through seven innings.

The new age of pitching specialization is often credited to Bucky Harris, the playing manager and so-called Boy Wonder of Washington. In 1924, trying to combat the Yankees' version of "five o'clock lightning" (games started late to accommodate stockbrokers), Harris relied on the great Walter (Big Train) Johnson as his durable starting ace but he also used Firpo Marberry, a large Texan, in relief early and often—50 games, 15 starts, and 195⅓ innings.

"Harris also used Marberry as an intimidator," wrote the venerable Shirley Povich in the *Washington Post* in 1996. Povich knew the subject; he had been a boy wonder himself as a reporter back in 1924. "In 1925, starting nary a game, he set a league record by appearing in 55 contests," Povich continued, "and probably led the league in brush-backs, including a few that I remember that were aimed at Babe Ruth."

According to Povich, Harris inspired the Yankees' Miller Huggins to use Wilcy Moore, a thirty-year-old rookie, in 50 games in 1927, 38 of them in relief. Later the Yankees developed Johnny (Fireman) Murphy from 1932 to 1947, followed by Joe Page, a left-hander who helped win the 1947 World Series.

Specialization entered a new era in 1949 with the arrival of Casey Stengel, who was not afraid to match his left-handed hitters against right-handed pitchers, and vice versa. "McGraw platooned me," Stengel reasoned, neglecting to note that he had detested being left on the bench.

Stengel was not averse to using pinch-runners, defensive replacements, or even placing a good-hitting pitcher, Tommy Byrne, in the seventh position in the batting order (which annoyed the infielder who had to bat ninth).

The game continued to evolve in the postwar era, with durable pitchers like Jim Konstanty, Joe Black, Hoyt Wilhelm, Larry Sherry, Mike Marshall, Rollie Fingers, and Dennis Eckersley. Then came the subspecies of "long men" and "short men" who specialized in "holds" in the seventh and eighth innings, before the arrival of "closers" like Mariano Rivera of the Yankees.

The very best relief pitchers had their agents insert clauses into their contracts that guaranteed bonuses for a certain number of "saves," a new statistical category. These specialists normally were used only in "save" circumstances.

Defensive specialists, who sometimes answered to the nickname of "Leather," were throwbacks to the days when Sammy Byrd and other Yankee outfielders were known as "Babe Ruth's legs." Charles O. Finley once carried a pinch-runner, Herb Washington, who scored 33 runs in two seasons without ever batting or playing the field. Some catchers extended their careers by handling the erratic swerves of knuckleballers, while a veteran catcher like Tim McCarver remained valuable by having a rapport with a moody ace like Steve Carlton, who would pitch only to McCarver.

Sometimes officials tinkered with the height of the mound or the width of the strike zone, to produce more hits or fewer hits, depending on the impulse of the time. Some springs, umpires were given instructions to tighten up one rule or another, which meant the umps would spend the first few weeks of the season officiously calling balks or some such legality, until it was safe to go back to normalcy again.

The gifts of tactics and resourcefulness from the Negro Leagues just kept on giving. In the 1959 World Series, the Los Angeles Dodgers were led by Maury Wills, a minor league escapee who had discovered the ancient skill of stealing bases, and wise old Jim Gilliam, a former Negro Leaguer who batted second, often slapping the ball on the ground to move Wills along. The White Sox, with their shortstop and second baseman, Luis Aparacio and Nellie Fox, pretty much did the same. The Dodgers won a throwback Series that Wee Willie Keeler and Ty Cobb would have appreciated.

———

For all the changes, the game is held together by the rituals and records. No sport is so laced with statistics, many of them arcane, but some of them downright momentous—numbers with lives all their own. Baseball records are generally regarded as modern beginning with 1900 and the establishment of the two major leagues.

Collective wisdom says the greatest of all records is Joe DiMaggio's streak of hitting in 56 consecutive games in 1941, a tribute to DiMaggio's great consistency (to say nothing of his speed, power, and skill). The closest anybody has come to DiMaggio's record was 44, set by Willie Keeler in the pre-modern year of 1897 and Pete Rose in 1978.

However, Frank Robinson, the great slugger and a manager of four teams, has often marveled at another statistic—DiMaggio's matching career totals of 361 home runs and 369 strikeouts, an amazing ratio between power and discipline. (Robinson, hardly a free swinger, hit 586 home runs and struck out 1,532 times.)

One record that seemed out of sight was Lou Gehrig's streak of 2,130 consecutive games, halted only by the detection of his fatal illness, but Cal Ripken, Jr., played in 2,632 straight before sitting out a game in 1998. Ripken had insisted on playing day-in, day-out, sometimes clearly needing a rest from an injury or grueling cross-country road trip.

The old sports cliché that records are made to be broken was tested in 1961 when Roger Maris hit 61 homers in the 162-game season, thereby breaking Babe Ruth's total of 60, but then Mark McGwire and Sammy Sosa raced past Ruth and Maris in the giddy season of 1998, later to be tainted by suspicions that players had been chemically enlarged during that era. McGwire's total of 70 homers in 1998 was itself eclipsed by Barry Bonds's 73 in 2001, but Bonds's subsequent connection to a grand jury investigation into body-building drugs eventually brought more respect back to Ruth and Maris and Henry Aaron. Another memorable statistic was Ruth's 714 career home runs—until Aaron passed it en route to setting the record at 755, while receiving sackloads of racist hate mail.

Some pitching records will never be approached because of the way the game has evolved, with late-inning specialists and limitations on pitch counts. Cy Young's 511 career victories are untouchable and so are his 749 complete games along with Grover Cleveland Alexander's 90 career shutouts, tributes to a vanished age. In more modern times, Nolan Ryan pitched from 1966 to 1993, striking out 5,714 batters and pitching seven no-hitters, three more than Sandy Koufax.

Ty Cobb's 1915 record for stolen bases held up for decades, until 1962, when Maury Wills stole 104. Lou Brock advanced the record to 118 in 1974 and Rickey Henderson stole 130 in 1982. Henderson was so obsessed with his records that sometimes he would stop at second base rather than take a chance trying for a triple, knowing he could steal third base a minute or two later. Pete Rose's record for total games, 3,562, and his record for total hits, 4,256, could last as long as his ban for gambling—that is to say, forever.

———

Even the shape and function of the ballparks seemed to go in cycles. The ancient ballparks had been eccentric, squeezed onto plots of land in the old cities, but the new stadiums of the late 1960s were designed to accommodate both baseball and football, which meant they were blandly circular in shape, enclosed, uninteresting, often with artificial turf. These came to be known as "cookie-cutter" stadiums.

There was only one cathedral in baseball, the majestic Yankee

Stadium, which was remodeled in the 1970s and ultimately turned into a sort of electric church, replete with noise and glitter. The architectural trend of the 1990s was unabashed homage to the old days, celebrating the enduring intimate scale of Chicago's Wrigley Field and Boston's Fenway Park by erecting new places with idiosyncratic nooks and crannies, retro brick and grillwork, open spaces to provide a glimpse of downtown. Even though a large segment of the American population had moved to suburbia and exurbia (at least the white population, still the core of the game's support), the new ballparks flourished in the hearts of the cities. It was still an urban game.

These new stadiums contained huge amounts of luxury boxes, with air-conditioning, private bathrooms, refrigerators, and television sets, virtually guaranteeing that some well-heeled patrons could stay inside, near the cheese dip, never actually having to watch the game.

Among the variations in the new places was SkyDome in Toronto (never "the" SkyDome), thirty-one stories high, with a retractable roof that could close down in a quarter of an hour, and a hotel behind the center-field stands. Another variation was Oriole Park at Camden Yards in downtown Baltimore, with an old brick factory behind right field and delicatessen and microbrew stands in an outdoor food court. In Cleveland's Jacobs Field, pedestrians could watch a game in progress through an iron fence behind left field. The scaled-down 1996 Olympic Stadium in Atlanta promptly became Turner Field (not Henry Aaron Field, as many had hoped). Seattle's dismal Kingdome was imploded, replaced by Safeco Field, with a roof that could be wheeled out in case of rain.

As appealing as they were, many of the new ballparks were plagued by the corporate names attached to them. Dot-com companies temporarily awash in money paid millions of dollars for "naming rights," attaching geeky corporate names to the stadiums. San Diego's stadium, named for a civic treasure—sportswriter Jack Murphy, who had campaigned for a major league franchise—was renamed for a computer-age company, but the stadium itself was soon replaced by another ballpark. In a bizarre trend in all the major sports in North America, many of the nouveau holders of naming rights went bankrupt, some spectacularly. For example, Houston's new open-air downtown ballpark was tainted by the name Enron Field for months after the scandalous collapse of that company, the large letters taunting investors and employees who had believed in the fraudulent dream. Misfortune continued to strike companies that had purchased naming rights; some kind of righteous Ruthian hex was suspected.

XVIII

WHO'S IN CHARGE?

The day came when baseball began hearing footsteps—large, loud footsteps. The National Football League took off in the 1950s, as network television brought the sport, previously more popular on the college level, to all corners of the country. Life in America slowed down on Sunday afternoons as fans crowded into dens or bars.

Some people say that football achieved parity on Sunday, December 28, 1958, when the Baltimore Colts won the championship by defeating the New York Giants, 23–17, in overtime, in what is still called "The Greatest Game Ever Played."

But football's defining moment probably arrived in 1962, when the club owners dealt with the reality of network television revenue. The Giants, a landmark franchise that had struggled for decades just to get New Yorkers to buy tickets, were now being paid $175,000 a season by the CBS network while the Green Bay Packers, another old-time franchise in a small city in northern Wisconsin, were being paid only $35,000.

It was clear, based on viewers and population, that the larger franchises would dominate and eventually force out the lesser franchises. But Wellington Mara, the patriarch of the Giants, spoke up that day for tradition and solidarity.

"Well argued that the N.F.L. was only as strong as its weakest link, that Green Bay should receive as much money as any of the other teams," Pete Rozelle, the commissioner at the time, later recalled. When Mara spoke, other owners listened, agreeing to spread the network payments equally, ensuring a level playing field in subsequent contracts with the networks. Although some owners would move their franchises, sometimes defying the league to stop them, there was an almost universal sense of stewardship.

By the 1966 season, after making peace with a rival league, football had a championship game, eventually called the Super

Bowl and measured in Roman numerals. Before he died in 2005, Wellington Mara would watch his Giants win two Super Bowls, while tiny Green Bay, able to spend equal network swag on players, would win the first two championships as well as Super Bowl XXXI after the 1996 season. By then, pro football had the television ratings to claim it was the most popular sport, at least around weekends during the season. Baseball's mythic, psychic hold might still be deeper than football's—but hardly anybody held World Series parties the way they did Super Bowl parties.

The difference between football and baseball goes beyond the way the sports divide their television revenue. Football's money comes mostly from a network contract while baseball teams mostly make money from their local cable contracts. One can only imagine if baseball owners had demonstrated the statesmanship of Wellington Mara at key moments in their history.

Instead, baseball has a tradition of fractiousness, going back to John J. McGraw's petulant refusal to let his Giants participate in a World Series in 1904. The bitterness between Ban Johnson's American League and the National League led directly to the White Sox scandal of 1919. The favorable 1922 Supreme Court decision, while greatly appreciated by the avaricious owners, only encouraged them to act for themselves, which came quite naturally.

Many of the old-time baseball owners were not all that different from the football owners. They had come along when their livelihood depended on persuading a few hundred extra fans to pay their way into their rudimentary ballparks early in the century. The Griffiths, Macks, and Comiskeys had morphed from players to owners; the Stonehams had owned the Giants for decades. Even the owners who came with outside wealth tended to be hands-on control freaks who needed to be a major part of the show—autocratic, flamboyant, visionary, or stupid, but often dedicated to the sport. If there was one owner who had the ear of the others, it was Walter O'Malley, but his power was derived from the owners' fear and awe of him rather than from any sense of collegiality.

With football (and later pro basketball and auto racing) putting the squeeze on baseball, the old breed of owners was being forced out. Owners now needed tax lawyers and contract lawyers to help them run a ball club, and they also needed deep pockets from some significant outside business. They became virtually minority partners with the television networks and growing cable companies, who told them what time to play their games—and how many minutes were needed between innings to sell the sponsor's soft drinks or cars.

One owner realized he was a dinosaur. Bill Veeck had surfaced once again with the White Sox, in 1975, putting into practice the showmanship theories he had elucidated in his classic book, *Veeck as in Wreck*. But Veeck could see he was not going to thrive in this new age. He hated corporate boxes that catered to expense-account types rather than Veeck's democratic ideal of real fans and he also had a healthy (but outdated and self-defeating) disinterest in television.

The last days of Veeck are remembered for the singular disaster of Anti-Disco Night in 1979, a brilliant idea concocted by his aspiring showman son, Mike, that involved fans turning in their vinyl records as a statement against disco music—reasonable enough, on the surface, but with one major flaw: after a few beers, thousands of fans felt the need to sail the records onto the field, thereby causing the White Sox to lose the game by forfeit. Veeck soon sold the Sox to Jerry Reinsdorf and Eddie Einhorn, both better suited for the television age.

Other familiar names began to fade out: Stoneham in San Francisco, the Griffith family in Minnesota, Finley in Oakland. The new breed of owner with corporate backing included Ted Turner, the brash proprietor of WTBS, a superstation that beamed the Braves all over North America. Turner overspent and underachieved with the Braves, once naming himself the manager for a day, until Commissioner Kuhn put an end to that. The Braves reached the postseason exactly once from 1975 through 1990, and Turner bragged of losing millions of dollars. But as sometimes happens with eccentrics like Turner, with that strange look in his eye, he possessed an inner wisdom. At the same time he was being ridiculed for losing money and games, Turner was underwriting 162 games a year—he was subsidizing programming for his vast network.

Turner was a visionary, the only baseball owner I ever met who would lecture about the need to get along with the Soviet Union ("my pinko Commie buddies") and save the world's environment ("but what about the elephants!"). The public practically laughed in his face, yet he was brilliant.

The owners had a consistent management problem. They could not keep good help. Their erratic, selfish ways kept them from imposing any rational business order on the people they hired to run their business. Ban Johnson, now largely forgotten, was more powerful than the owners he had pulled together to start the American League. There would never be another like him.

There would never be another Judge Landis, either, which is probably a good thing. He was hired on the dubious but classically American premise that baseball needed an authority figure, the hangin' judge, who arrives in the last reel of the western movie and executes all the bad guys. Considering that the frontier had just closed, America was still hankering for a leader who could wield a mighty six-shooter, or maybe just a gavel. Judge Landis gave that impression in 1915 with his favorable decision limiting the Federal League. He pleased the owners as a judge and he continued to please the owners as commissioner, making an example of all eight White Sox players, despite their highly varied degrees of guilt.

Sounding like a populist but probably just doing the bidding of the lazier owners, he tried to squash Branch Rickey's farm system. No doubt expressing his own as well as most owners' essential racial views, he fought off attempts to hire black players in the early 1940s. Yet Kenesaw Mountain Landis survived because the public and the owners felt he looked just like a commissioner judge should look—white, male, tousled head of white hair, and not a shred of indecision or ambiguity to him. Complexity makes folks nervous in these here parts.

The worst thing about Judge Landis's twenty-four-year rule was that he propagated a myth that the commissioner exists for the general good of baseball. Sometimes the commissioners even believed this job description themselves, which was dangerous to their job tenure. The reality is that the commissioner serves the owners. He is their man. And unless they come up with a job description and goals, his task is virtually impossible.

Landis's successor, Albert D. (Happy) Chandler, from the Bluegrass region of Kentucky, was a progressive for his time and place. He could sing "My Old Kentucky Home" in a sweet, quavering tenor, and never forgot a name or a face. In his new job, Happy Chandler had only to remember sixteen, yet he probably lost a few immediately by his brave stand of championing the inclusion of blacks in the major leagues and he soon displeased a majority of owners and was dismissed in 1951.

Ford Frick, the former newspaperman, replaced Chandler, fully understanding he was there to serve the owners, which he did, from 1951 through 1965. When Frick bowed out, the owners hired an anonymous Air Force general, William D. Eckert, apparently confusing him with another general named Zuckert. As the New York sportswriter Larry Fox wrote the day Eckert was chosen, "Jeez. They went and got the unknown soldier." Lacking any knowledge of baseball, Eckert did nothing to challenge the owners, but he was let go anyway, in 1968, followed by Bowie K. Kuhn, the former counsel to baseball. Kuhn had been a scoreboard operator at Washington's Griffith Stadium as a boy and genuinely loved the game, but he came along at the worst possible time. Marvin Miller of the Players Association began hitting Kuhn's legal pitches as if it were batting practice, and the owners banished Kuhn in 1984.

The choice for Kuhn's replacement was so logical it was doomed to failure. Peter Ueberroth, a former travel agency executive, had just presided over the 1984 Summer Games in Los Angeles, using existing facilities, negotiating hard contracts, and turning profits of over $225 million to a foundation for youth sports. Ueberroth, the first businessman ever to be commissioner, did not know much about baseball but he knew about budgets and staffing and labor costs. It made him totally crazy when the club owners could not evoke the same business sense that had obviously served many of them well in their original businesses.

Ueberroth's hardest challenge in Los Angeles had been the boycott by Soviet-bloc nations. As commissioner, Ueberroth would soon come to think of the boycott as the good old days. Unhindered by any great sentimentality for the game itself, he tried to consolidate the balkanized business practices of baseball, but antagonized the rich and independent cusses who ran the teams. He soon realized that the owners from the huge cable television markets would not find a way to share the swag with owners in the lesser cable markets, thereby creating an inequity on the field, presumably forever.

A short strike in August of 1985 ended only when Lee MacPhail, the son of Larry and one of the most respected officials in baseball, brought the sides together. On March 31, 1989, Ueberroth's term ended and he walked away from the owners' scorn with a feeling that was quite mutual.

The owners then turned to A. Bartlett Giamatti, scholar, writer, former president of Yale University, and full-fledged Red Sox fan. Giamatti was no stranger to labor strife at Yale but as commissioner he inherited an issue he took highly personally—Pete Rose's denial that he had gambled on baseball. Days after banishing Rose, Giamatti died of a heart attack on September 1, 1989, after only five months as commissioner. Fay Vincent, a former executive of Columbia Pictures and Coca-Cola, and a close friend of Giamatti, took over as commissioner. Used to dealing with corporate boards, Vincent had never encountered anything quite like the squabbling disparate owners. He presided over the Bay Area earthquake in October of 1989, but was ousted by the owners on September 7, 1992.

For nearly six years, Allan H. (Bud) Selig, a former automobile dealer and the owner of the Milwaukee Brewers, served as interim commissioner. It was impossible to miss Selig's love for the game as he talked about how his mother had taken him from Milwaukee to New York on pilgrimages to Ebbets Field or Yankee Stadium. As commissioner, he was faced with contemporary problems like labor negotiations, shaky franchises, drug and steroid issues, and the imbalance of cable television revenues, praised by many fellow owners as a problem-solver but perceived by press and public as somewhat of a ditherer.

In 1994, the owners vowed they would never again be beaten in contract negotiations. Selig wrung his hands and professed sadness at the work stoppage that summer but Donald Fehr, the head of the Players Association, skipped the niceties and said baseball would be back when the players were satisfied. For the first time since 1904, when McGraw had refused to play nicely with the American League, there was no World Series, leaving a terrible gap in the hearts of hard-core fans.

The players gained another contractual victory in the spring of 1995, and went back to work in a slightly shortened season. On July 9, 1998, Selig was officially named commissioner. He did not have an easy task. While attendance had tripled from 1964 to 2000, baseball was losing public attention to football, basketball, golf, and NASCAR. Children were playing soccer in youth leagues or skateboarding, and then going home to huddle over computer games. Some owners began paying for a portion of their new palaces, but other towns could not arrange financing for stadiums. Montreal, once a vibrant baseball city, lost its Expos to Washington in 2005.

Selig delivered a mixed message, raving about high attendance but talking about eliminating two or four teams, using the ominous word "contracting," which sounded like something out of *The Sopranos.* ("Hey, Bud, you want us to contract the Twins or the Devil Rays?") For all of Selig's fretting, the value of clubs continued to rise, even after factoring in inflation. For example: the small-market Kansas City Royals had been worth an entry fee of $5.35 million in the expansion draft of 1968 but were sold for $96 million in 2000.

Even the Los Angeles Dodgers were sold. Walter O'Malley had bought out Branch Rickey's one-quarter share in Brooklyn in 1950 for $1.05 million. In 1998, his son Peter sold the franchise, for estate-planning purposes, to Rupert Murdoch, the Australian-born news baron, for $311 million. The Murdochites made a mess of the gloried Dodgers, and the team was sold again, still worth a fortune because of Walter O'Malley's land deals in the 1950s.

The commissioner's job seemed to be to plead poverty, while presiding over expensive transfers of owners, some of whom had cable money to spend. The owners did slap luxury taxes on their highest spenders and distributed the money to poorer clubs in a primitive attempt to stop the worst recidivists among themselves from spending so much money. Yet spend they did.

The world had grown complicated. Like all commissioners, Selig was overshadowed by the Landis Syndrome, the national anticipation that a commissioner would come stalking into his box seat wearing a black jurist's robe, shaking a magisterial mane, pounding a gavel, shouting, "Off with their heads!" The eighty-year chasm between high expectations of commissioners and the dysfunction of the owners would soon lead to highly public embarrassment.

XIX

FOUR SCANDALS

T he funniest thing I ever saw in baseball was Pete Rose's green-ies kicking in during a rain delay," a former teammate once said, evoking a vision of Rose's stocky body bouncing off the club-house walls, with no outlet for his chemically induced energy.

As a young reporter, I encountered players unaccountably jab-bering in the minutes before a game. One of the most competitive players I ever met used to excuse himself before the game so he could drink "a major-league cup of coffee," which, I have since come to understand, refers to a mixture of black coffee and green-ies, or amphetamines. Eventually, the clubhouse doors were closed an hour before game time, so players could have time to, as the say-ing goes, "prepare."

And then there was a night exhibition in Florida a long time ago, when I watched a pitcher who was trying to hang on in the majors, lurching around the mound, like a sailor in a hurricane. He fired so many wild pitches in the general vicinity of home plate that the crusty old manager had to trudge out to the mound and remove him from the game. Later that night I asked the pitcher what the problem had been, and he made a flicking motion with his hand, like a man tossing pills down his gullet. Some hyper people are just not cut out for greenies.

Since I did not report this little scene back then—the pitcher was a friend of mine—it is probably unfair to say the commissioner of the day should have done something about it. It is safe to say there is a long tradition of stimulants in major league clubhouses, and that nobody wanted to know.

By the early 1980s, the dysfunction in management and the standoff with the Players Association would lead to four scandals, all of them comparable to the disaster of 1919, when the Black Sox were throwing the World Series but owners and officials were pow-erless to intervene.

The first scandal was the prevalence of so-called recreational drugs among the players, whose salaries had leaped to unimaginable heights. Baseball still lagged far behind many American industries in the treatment of chemical and alcohol addiction. It was not until 1980 that players like Darrell Porter and Bob Welch talked openly about having gone through rehabilitation centers. One of the problems was that baseball people tended to regard chemical addiction as outright subversive while alcohol was regarded as a traditional way of relaxing. "Heck, he can have a beer or two," one prominent manager insisted about a player of his who had acknowledged being an alcoholic.

Drugs were, of course, against the law. In 1983, twenty major league players were named in a drug case in Kansas City, Missouri, in which four Royals went to jail: Willie Wilson, Willie Aikens, Jerry Martin, and Vida Blue. For a brief time under Kuhn, there was an agreement that clubs could request testing for cocaine, but marijuana, amphetamines, and alcohol were not included. That policy expired in October of 1985.

The plague of drugs stopped being funny when players began losing their skills at an early age, right in front of our eyes. Every team seemed to have somebody with marvelous skills who suddenly turned into a clumsy and inarticulate hulk, no longer able to find first base without a Boy Scout guide.

Marvin Miller, the longtime leader of the Players Association, once described uppers and downers laid out "like jelly beans" in clubhouses.

"Who supplied them?" Miller asked rhetorically in an interview in the *New York Times.* "Certainly not the players union. We didn't make much progress in the early 1980s because it wasn't seen as an issue. The owners definitely weren't pushing it."

In 1984, Peter Ueberroth came over from the Olympic movement, in which athletes faced regular testing and were banned for one positive drug test. He arrived just in time for a number of major-leaguers to be implicated in another drug case, this one in Pittsburgh. Keith Hernandez, who had been hastily traded to the Mets in 1983, testified in court that he had used cocaine while a member of the Cardinals, describing a widespread "romance" between players and drugs. "It was like a demon in me," Hernandez said.

Other players said they had easily obtained illegal drugs in the clubhouse in Pittsburgh. Two regulars on San Diego's 1984 league champions, Alan Wiggins and Eric Show, developed addictions and died young. Dwight Gooden and Darryl Strawberry helped the Mets win the World Series in 1986 but never fulfilled their Hall of Fame potential because of chemical and legal problems. When Olympic sports began random testing for drugs, Ueberroth called for mandatory testing starting in 1986, but Donald Fehr filed a grievance, citing the civil liberties of his clients, and the owners showed no stomach for that fight.

———

Ueberroth was present during another scandal involving the owners and the players, this one over the owners' limiting players' salaries. This practice was specifically banned by the 1985 Collective Bargaining Agreement, which included a provision that players "would not act collectively in any salary negotiation—and neither would the clubs." Ueberroth frequently lectured the owners not to spend wildly on free agents, but he always made sure to remind the owners to stay within the legal boundaries of the agreement.

Lee MacPhail, one of the solid figures in baseball and an advisor to Ueberroth, said, "We must rely on the unilateral, self-imposed restraints of each individual club to do what experience and reasonable expectations indicate is in its own best interest."

The owners, for once, took the advice more uniformly than anybody could have predicted. The most blatant example was Andre Dawson, a star in Montreal, who was eligible for free agency but could not get an offer until he agreed to sign a blank contract with the Cubs in 1987. Playing for an unreasonably low base salary of $500,000, Dawson hit 49 home runs and drove in 137 runs, although he did make extra money via incentive bonuses driving his earnings up to a still-ludicrous $700,000.

That was not good enough for the Players Association. Fehr and the players say they spent $4.6 million in legal costs to charge all the owners with illegally contriving to hold down salaries. The free agency era had demonstrated that baseball would not fall apart if the players moved to the highest bidder, and now the players had legal backup. An arbitrator in 1990 levied a $280 million penalty against all the owners in three cases, including Dawson's, of what the players call collusion, and the two sides settled on that amount. In 1998 President Clinton signed the Curt Flood Act, which gave players the same protection under antitrust laws that all other athletes enjoyed. This legislation revoked the old antitrust exemption only for labor relations but did not affect the owners' broad powers regarding relocation, expansion, or the minor leagues.

—

It was impossible to miss the insatiable self-involvement of Pete Rose, the chesty hometown hero of the Cincinnati Reds, who had willed himself to the record for base hits, held by Tyrus Raymond Cobb. (In his second marriage, Rose would name a son "Tyler" in homage to the ornery star he would surpass.)

For a very long time, Rose was "good for the game," a precious quality indeed. As millionaire players hid behind designer sunglasses, headsets, and protective agents, Rose was a gregarious presence at the ballpark, signing autographs for the fans, gossiping with the writers. Pete had an opinion about everything.

It was quite evident that Rose had a lusty appetite for various pleasures and diversions, including gambling. At the Florida racetracks and greyhound courses and jai-alai frontons, one could only wonder if there were three Peter Edward Roses, with his Prince Valiant haircut bobbing as he hustled between the seller's window and, occasionally, the cashier's window.

Management overlooked Rose's habits until very late in his career, when he came home as the Reds' player-manager. There were concerns that he was involved with steroid suppliers and bookmakers, betting on sports, maybe even his own, which was specifically banned, according to regulations printed in English and Spanish (and now in Japanese as well) on every clubhouse door.

Ueberroth hauled him in for a meeting, only to have Rose assure him he was not betting on baseball, absolutely not. Pete Rose would never do such a thing. When Ueberroth departed, Rose became the problem of Bart Giamatti, who regarded gambling, particularly government-operated lotteries, as a moral flaw. After investigators compiled a dossier on Rose, he stonewalled them in private confrontations.

Ultimately, in 1989, Giamatti and his lawyers persuaded Rose's lawyers to make Rose accept a lifetime ban from the game, with the written promise that he could reapply after one year. Perhaps Rose believed this scenario but, when his ban was announced in a major press conference, Giamatti, in response to a question, said he had "concluded" that Rose had bet on baseball, including the Reds. This public judgment was not part of the deal Rose had anticipated. Rose quickly realized he had been given the bum's rush out of the game.

Anybody who has ever dealt with addictive behavior could detect the blatant denial in Rose, but Giamatti seemed to take Rose's bluster personally, dismissing him in a fury. Giamatti went on vacation in New England and died of a heart attack eight days later, at the age of fifty-one. Rose was not always good at reading the racing charts but he could figure out there was only one way Giamatti's death was going to play out: Pete Killed Bart.

The next two commissioners, Fay Vincent and Bud Selig, remained staunchly in favor of a lifetime ban, at least unless Rose repented. Rose did not help himself through a decade of further denial and his five months in prison for tax evasion. He emerged as the star attraction at autograph shows, signing memorabilia, showing up in Cooperstown during the annual Hall of Fame bash, a seedy ghost who would not go away.

Rose haunted the game in 1999 when fans were asked to punch out computer cards to select a best-of-the-century team, in a promotion by a credit card company. To the chagrin of Selig, and just about everybody else, Rose was voted onto the team by a nation hooked on Las Vegas, office pools, and lotteries. When the thirty-man team was introduced during the World Series in Atlanta, Rose hustled in, appropriately enough, from Atlantic City, straight from an autograph bazaar, and immediately made a belligerent appearance on national television.

"Charles Manson can get a hearing," Rose told NBC reporter Jim Gray. "I hope they don't wait till 2060 to review my case." Charlie Hustle even upstaged the ailing Ted Williams during the introductions.

Years later, while promoting his book, Rose admitted he had bet on baseball, but by then even tolerant fans had lost sympathy with him. The public did not have any moral problem with his gambling, apparently, but now found him a bore. He realized he was facing a very long wait before any commissioner would ever reinstate him. Rose had wanted to become Ty Cobb. Instead he had become Shoeless Joe Jackson.

———

Head in the sand, baseball contributed to the drug epidemic, the collusion penalties, and the festering Rose problem. For a long time, the fourth scandal did not seem like a crisis at all, but rather a jubilee, a Fourth of July fireworks display, an exploding scoreboard's worth of home runs.

The owners did not want to know. Starting in the early 1990s, players became noticeably thicker in the shoulders, forearms, and necks. A willowy player could bid farewell to teammates at the end of the season and reappear the following spring with a physique most approximating the main character of the television series *The Incredible Hulk,* with mood swings to match. Facial bone structure seemed to change overnight, with jaws protruding to Cro-Magnon dimensions. Players coming out of the clubhouse shower would inadvertently display a raging case of acne on their backs, a telltale sign of steroid usage. But there was no testing for bodybuilding drugs, and everybody went along.

Many players openly used creatine, a bodybuilding substance not banned by baseball. I can still see a certain owner distributing creatine shakes to players in the center of the clubhouse during spring training. It was baseball's version of the Gold Rush.

The facile explanation is that management was looking for a quick fix of home runs after the labor stoppage of 1994–95, but just like the folk legend that baseballs were knowingly juiced up after the 1919 Black Sox scandal, the explanation is more complicated.

By the 1990s, the Silly Boys on the television sports shows were hung up on showing endless clips of home runs. The players were no fools. They wanted to be on the highlight films. You didn't get time on ESPN by dropping a perfect bunt.

Management was thrilled at the perfect antidote for the labor blues. In 1998, two sluggers, Mark McGwire of St. Louis and Sammy Sosa of the Cubs, chased the home run records of Babe Ruth and Roger Maris. Both were appealing in their own way, with McGwire somewhat intense and private and Sosa more gregarious, frequently waving to the fans.

One day, Steve Wilstein of the Associated Press was waiting to interview McGwire in front of his locker, a totally normal process in a sport that provides daily access before and after every game. Wilstein idly noticed a package labeled "androstenedione" in plain view on McGwire's shelf, and later he discovered this was a steroid-like substance that increased body mass and could be bought over the counter, and was not banned by baseball, but was outlawed in most Olympic sports.

After diligent reporting, Wilstein wrote about the stuff in McGwire's locker, prompting a furor. McGwire did not deny using andro, as it is known, but he did claim Wilstein had intruded on his privacy. McGwire wound up breaking the record and finishing the season with 70 home runs while Sosa hit 66, and both were given credit for "saving" baseball after the labor dispute. In fact, attendance had already surged upward after the stoppage.

Faced with public concern, McGwire soon announced he would no longer use androstenedione because it set a bad example to the youth of America, who were bulking up for sports and self-esteem but later facing emotional and physical dangers. His body no longer able to ward off injuries, McGwire retired after the 2001 season, but by that time he no longer held the home run record. Barry Bonds, son of a major-leaguer, hit 73 home runs that year, with his compact swing and marvelous discipline and a body that seemed vastly more muscular than the whippet-like frame of his early days.

With suspicion growing about Bonds, McGwire, and Sosa, Major League Baseball and the Players Association agreed to the first mandatory testing of drugs in the history of collective bargaining, but the testing was widely criticized for its limitations.

The association was forced on the defensive in spring training of 2003, when a young pitcher for Baltimore, Steve Bechler, died of heatstroke after a workout. It was later determined that Bechler, concerned about being overweight, had been taking an over-the-counter supplement that contained ephedrine, a diuretic used for weight loss. Ephedrine was already banned in college sports, the Olympics, and the National Football League. Congress quickly banned ephedrine, forcing management and the union to amend their agreement to include ephedrine, a highly unusual concession by the players.

Another disgrace followed. Under the new labor agreement, since more than 5 percent of the players had tested positive in 2003, public disclosure of violators and their penalties automatically went into effect.

Things got worse late in 2003, when word came out of northern California that a federal grand jury was investigating steroid and other drug usage by many prominent athletes with links to the Bay Area Laboratory Co-Operative (BALCO). The *San Francisco Chronicle* later revealed that Barry Bonds had told the grand jury in 2003 that he had received a clear substance and a cream from his personal trainer, and supplied by BALCO. Bonds claimed he had believed they were a nutritional supplement, flaxseed oil, and a balm for arthritis. The newspaper also claimed that prosecutors had found Bonds's name on a BALCO list, linking him with "human growth hormone, Depo-Testosterone, undetectable steroids known as 'the cream' and 'the clear,' insulin and Clomid, a drug for female infertility sometimes used to enhance the effect of testosterone."

The newspaper also claimed that Jason Giambi of the Yankees had testified in December of 2003 that he had injected himself with human growth hormone and had also used steroids as early as 2001.

These revelations put intense pressure on Donald Fehr, who had been serving as an advisor to the United States Olympic Committee while that organization was trying to combat drugs, yet at the same time Fehr had steadfastly resisted significant testing for his clients in the Players Association. As the BALCO scandal deepened, Fehr left his advisory post with the USOC.

The embarrassment only got worse for Selig and Fehr. On March 17, 2005, a congressional subcommittee held a long day of hearings into steroid usage. After gripping testimony from several parents whose athlete sons had committed suicide during withdrawal from steroids, an international drug expert, Dr. Gary I. Wadler, described an epidemic of a million youths using steroids without medical supervision.

Nobody came off well in the afternoon hearing. Jose Canseco, a retired slugger, reiterated charges in his book that he and several other players in the room had used steroids. Sosa said little, retreating behind the use of a translator. McGwire, badgered by legislators to discuss his possible use of bodybuilding drugs, abjectly replied he did not want to delve into the past. Curt Schilling, a pitcher who had been billed as the hearing's star critic of steroids, managed to look ridiculous by testifying that he actually did not know much at all. And Rafael Palmeiro, a hitter with Hall of Fame statistics, wagged his finger at the members of Congress and said that despite Canseco's charges, "I have never used steroids—period."

The mood became even more acrimonious in a late-afternoon session when members of the subcommittee ridiculed Selig and Fehr for their bland answers about drug usage. The members of Congress had started out the long day fawning over the celebrities and expressing their undying love for the national game. By the end of the day they were threatening the entire industry with an antisteroid law if baseball did not wise up.

The public scolding was the best thing that ever could have happened to Allan H. Selig. Over the years, management had taken a series of lickings from Miller and Fehr in private negotiations, but now the members of Congress had publicly given Selig orders to fight back. In front of a separate committee a few months later, Fightin' Bud came out firmly in favor of tougher testing and tougher penalties.

On July 1, 2005, the finger-waving Palmeiro tested positive for stanozolol, a bodybuilding steroid that is almost always taken via injection, and not accidentally as part of a medication or vitamin supplement. Palmeiro was suspended for the maximum 10 games but his reputation was shattered, his Hall of Fame aspirations in jeopardy.

Bonds sat out most of the 2005 season because his injured knee did not respond to surgery and rehabilitation, but he returned in 2006; although he was considerably slowed down by age and injuries, he passed Ruth's old home run record of 714 in late May and trudged after Aaron's mark of 755. Bonds soon discovered that the rules had changed.

After the intense criticism from Congress, management and the players had accepted a three-strikes-and-out policy for 2006, with penalties of 50- and 100-game suspensions for the first two offenses, followed by a lifetime suspension for the third, bringing baseball in line with the general drug policies of most other sports, and sending the message to young people not to start using illegal drugs to bulk up. As usual, baseball had reacted to a crisis rather than anticipating it.

With critical books and articles starting to come out about Bonds, Major League Baseball and even his own team seemed to tiptoe around him. Bonds claimed he was a victim of racial prejudice because he was African-American, insisting that baseball had shown little stomach for going after the white McGwire and the Latino Sosa during their peak years. More to the point, Bonds had the misfortune of still being active when circumstances and legal investigations caught up with baseball, and perhaps even with him.

Selig, who had presided so happily over the home run festivals a few years earlier, was now under huge public pressure to do something. He appointed a former senator, George Mitchell, to lead an investigation into steroid usage in the sport. Facing severe penalties for testing positive, the post-2005 players seemed to get smaller before our eyes, as if magically reversing the previous generation of muscle development. Baseball had also been forced to test for amphetamines for the first time, ushering in an entirely new chemical era.

With McGwire already retired, and with Sosa and Palmeiro unsigned in 2006, Bonds was out there by himself, while the public debated whether the four of them might lose popularity as well as votes for the Hall of Fame when they became eligible five years after their respective retirements. Some sports reporters said they might withhold votes for these sluggers as a gesture of criticism. While my employer, the *New York Times,* does not permit reporters to vote for any award—a sensible policy, since the *Times* wants us to report news, not make it—we are allowed to express our opinions. My own reaction is that the commissioner and the union ducked drug testing for a generation, making it legally impossible to penalize players who were never tested.

The records must stand because there is no way to quantify how many home runs were hit by players who were on the stuff. Beyond the legalities, fans will always have their suspicions. Time and public opinion will judge Barry Bonds, who was a superb player as a slender youth and as a hulking elder. He will always walk under a cloud. Those suspicions seem quite enough.

XX

OCTOBER EXORCISMS

Like a drunk pedestrian weaving across eight lanes of traffic and making it to the other side, baseball has survived. Somehow, people always seem to know how the team of their youth is doing, seem to know when the World Series is taking place. Like the moon, sometimes hidden behind clouds yet directing the tides, baseball ritual exerts a territorial, ancestral pull. The World Series is the equivalent of a full moon: emotions tend to run at flood tide or ebb tide.

The game still flows the way it did for our elders, from winter gossip to spring training, mercifully in February, to warm summer night games to nippy autumn championship games. It all feels right, progressing from the familiar to the familiar, but producing gasps of surprise.

Casey Stengel, that grand old baseball man, used to rasp his theory that "Every day in baseball you see something you never saw before." The Old Man was right, as always. Just when it seems the owners or the players (or the fans, or the media, or the umpires) have bungled something irrevocably, the game itself surprises and delights, within the context of the old ways of doing things.

In the quickening weather of September—time running out, nippy drizzle, men in satiny team jackets peering owlishly out of crowded dugouts—fans in the twenty-first century follow the division races, informed by genetic imprints of ancient pennant races. If only by collective memory, fans have been through this group experience of epic victories and ghastly collapses. In these new days, the fans crane their necks toward the out-of-town scoreboards, following games all over the league (when the commercial-laden "message boards" bother to give scores, that is). The players claim they do not watch the scoreboard, but of course they lie.

Pennant races once were all-or-nothing propositions, producing exactly one champion per league. That ancient process was altered by division races, starting in 1969, and then in 1995 the owners expanded to a third round, adding a wild card team to three division champions. Even with the wild card gimmick, the races are heightened by more than a century of daily action, none of this once-a-week business of football.

Pennant races touch every team, even ones that are rarely in contention. Every franchise has a history of spoiling an entire season for some contender with hopes and dreams. That can be great fun, too.

Teams making a late-season run are compared to the 1914 Boston Braves, who roared from last to first place in the final months, or the sad-sack 1964 Phillies, who blew a lead of 6½ games with 12 games left, or the 1978 Yankees, who overcame a 13½-game lead by the Red Sox. But the most intense race of all came in 1951 when the New York Giants came from 13½ games behind in mid-August to catch their hated rivals—and, yes, they were hated—the Brooklyn Dodgers, winning a best-of-three playoff series on Bobby Thomson's home run, still the most dramatic homer ever hit in the very long history of this sport.

Sometimes latter-day races refer back to an epic pitching duel, like the one on October 8, 1908, when Mordecai (Three-Finger) Brown of the Cubs came out of the bullpen to beat Christy Mathewson of the Giants to decide the pennant. Decades later, weary aces like Randy Johnson of the 1995 Mariners saved an entire season with a creaky, painful, dramatic appearance in relief, evoking historical references to Three-Finger Brown, so long ago.

Even with modern lights and drainage, threatening weather sometimes revives references to 1938, when Gabby Hartnett of the Cubs hit a home run at dusk to help win a pennant. Whenever teams are still in contention in the final weekend, somebody harks back to 1949, when the Yankees beat the Red Sox twice to reach the World Series, or 1950, when Richie Ashburn of the Phillies threw out Cal Abrams of the Dodgers at home plate, and then Dick Sisler (son of George) hit a homer to clinch the pennant for the one-shot Philadelphia Whiz Kids.

The intra-league series that began in 1969 has produced its own genre of thrills and terror, most notably 1986, when the Red Sox came from a 3–1 deficit to beat the Angels in the American League and the Mets held off the Astros in a 16-inning sixth game to win the National League pennant. Gene Mauch, who managed the 1964 Phillies and the 1982 and 1986 Angels, had the terrible karma of faltering all three times. That would be the way he was identified in his 2005 obituaries: Manager Never Reached World Series.

Older fans have fading memories of the World Series as a sun-dappled exercise in early October, but nowadays, the Series seems under siege, starting after eight o'clock in chilly late October, basically unavailable to children back east or even adults who fall asleep by the middle innings.

Major League Baseball does its best to adulterate its own show-case event, lumping all statistics into "postseason records" that cut into the special quality of the World Series. Somehow the World Series survives.

Most World Series have been memorable for one thing or the other, or just for adding more records, more depth, more history, to the century-old institution. Every fan could come up with a totally arbitrary list of great World Series:

Mathewson's three shutouts in six days in 1905; a bad bounce over the Giants' third baseman in 1924 that gave Washington its only championship; Enos Slaughter's romp home to give the Cards a seventh-game victory over the Red Sox in 1946; Al Gionfriddo's catch on Joe DiMaggio and Cookie Lavagetto's two-out, pinch-hit, game-winning double to break up a walk-plagued no-hit effort by Bill Bevens as the Dodgers beat the Yankees in the 1947 fourth game; clutch hits by the journeyman Dusty Rhodes as the 1954 Giants swept Cleveland; the biblical Next Year that finally arrived in 1955 as Johnny Podres beat the Yanks in the Stadium, and church bells tolled all over Brooklyn; Bill Mazeroski's homer to abruptly win the 1960 Series for the Pirates; Brooks Robinson's glove at third base for the Orioles in 1970; Carlton Fisk's body-English homer to end the sixth game in damp Fenway Park, although the Reds would beat Boston in the seventh game; Reggie Jackson's bat in 1977 and 1978 (has there ever been a better nickname than Mr. October?); a two-out rally that ended with Mookie Wilson's grounder slipping through Bill Buckner's legs in 1986, before the Mets won the seventh game, too; like a throwback to Matty and Cy Young, Jack Morris pitching a 10-inning shutout as the Twins beat the Braves in 1991.

The World Series was mourned during the 1994 labor stoppage, and the Yankees' renaissance in 1996 made it seem like the old days had returned. But in the new century, the World Series produced surprises every year.

2001: Weeks after the terrorist attack, in a tense Yankee Stadium, President Bush jauntily jogged to the mound to throw out the first ball, with an imposing phalanx of armed troops clustered in the corridors behind the dugout. The Yankees won two games on home runs with two outs, which had never happened before in the Series, but a young franchise, Arizona, won two games at home for its first championship.

2002: The hard-luck club that had never reached the World Series, the Angels from Orange County, California, held off the Giants for their first championship, with the snakebit former manager, Gene Mauch, in secluded attendance. Although the Disney empire now owned the Angels, Jackie Autry, the widow of the beloved former owner, Gene Autry, was allowed to accept the trophy.

2003: A retread septuagenarian, Jack McKeon, came back to manage the Florida Marlins during the season and promptly beat the Yankees in their own stadium to win the Series. For the second time in six years, the Marlins would sell off their best players after winning a World Series.

2004: Babe Ruth, dead since 1948, was a living presence, with Boston fans wearing Red Sox jerseys that said "RUTH 3" on the back, a total anomaly, since numbers and names had never been displayed on uniforms when the Babe played for the Sox. But never mind. A rock band in the stands blared the modern version of "Tessie," the theme song during the Sox victory in the very first Series in 1903.

As the Sox played the Yankees in the league series, every fan in the two historic stadiums knew the Sox had not won a Series since 1918, before Babe Ruth was given away. The fans were thoroughly familiar with the history of Joe DiMaggio, Bucky Dent, Aaron Boone, Harry

Frazee, Ted Williams, Bill Buckner, and so on. When the Sox lost the first three games to the Yankees, it seemed like yet another gloomy chapter in the perhaps overwrought legend of the departed Babe, but then the Sox promptly swept the Yankees four straight, introducing uncharacteristic joy to dank old New England.

On the day before the Red Sox were to meet the Cardinals in what was universally taken as a replay of the unforgettable 1946 Series, Johnny Pesky popped into Fenway Park to pick up his Series tickets. The shortstop who had handled the tardy relay during Country Slaughter's romp was still active as a coach-emeritus, at eighty-five, with his own uniform and his own locker in the same miserable little clubhouse where he and Williams had dressed in 1946.

Pesky paused in front of his locker to answer a few questions about Slaughter's dash, fifty-eight years earlier. Once again, baseball's timeless detail was easily recalled from memory bank and record book. You could, as always, look it up.

"Slaughter was always good to me," Pesky said to a knot of reporters, some of them barely a quarter his age. "He always said he knew who was in center field"—meaning Slaughter had knowingly exploited the late-inning substitute, not Dominic DiMaggio, not Pesky.

The old boy was chipper and optimistic. If the Sox were to win the Series, Pesky promised, "I'm gonna take off all my clothes and run around the ballpark. Then I can die happy. Not that I'm going to die. I mean, I am going to die. But not soon."

Be assured there is no other sport in which an eighty-five-year-old relic-coach can banter about frolicking naked. The great bond between locker room chatter and the public ear was holding up. All of us standing around old Needlenose (Ted Williams's affectionate nickname for Pesky) delighted in being in the presence of so much living history, some angst but considerably more zest, from the daily ritual of this game.

The Red Sox did win. Four straight over the Cardinals. There is no report of Johnny Pesky running naked around Fenway—thank goodness for that—but various specters (or theories about specters) went scampering toward oblivion. Maybe the ghost of the Babe had not haunted the Red Sox for all those decades, but the 2004 World Series was one heck of an exorcism, all the same.

2005: Given the Northeast literary establishment's affection for the Red Sox, nothing could ever match the love-sonnet perfection of the Sox' reversal of misfortune. Such was the common wisdom until, in their own unlovely straightforward Midwestern way, the Chicago White Sox dealt with their own local demons the very next October.

The White Sox are not even the cutest ball team in their own town, that honor going to the Cubbies of the North Side, proving that once again location is everything. The White Sox battled two obstacles—their base on the déclassé South Side and their having gone without a championship since the gambling scandal of 1919. Since then, the White Sox had played in exactly one World Series, 1959, rarely touching off poetic impulse or widespread cultism. With an African-American general manager out of Stanford, Ken Williams, and a bilingual Venezuelan chatterbox manager, Ozzie Guillen, the Sox were a team after the Pan-American heart, although the world was slow to grasp that. Fans barely had time to mull the sad permanent exile of Shoeless Joe Jackson that hung over the Sox before they dismantled the Houston Astros in four straight games.

By the time the Sox were accorded a parade in Chicago, fans in other regions were just catching on to what a sweet, cathartic triumph this had been, very much like the Red Sox' sweep the year before, only with a beer toast rather than Merlot. As sport or spectacle, perhaps the 2005 Series was not compelling, but as an exorcism of yet another ghost it was sensationally appropriate. The ancient ritual of baseball had come through again.

EPILOGUE

Recently, I heard that my youngest brother, Christopher Vecsey, Ph.D., now a graying chaired professor, still plays baseball.

Yes, Chris told me, but it's the other American bat-and-ball game, the one called town ball, which was long ago swallowed up by the New York game, with its nine fielders and four bases, now played in expensive ballparks around the globe.

Town ball lives—not just as history but as frolic—in the annual Fourth of July picnic in the lovely little town of Hamilton, New York, not far from Cooperstown, the spurious home of baseball.

"We play on one of Colgate's grassy fields," Chris wrote in an e-mail. "A local doctor—Richard Cohen, GP, Little League umpire, Twins fan—organizes the game as part of the overall town celebration: parade down Broad Street, concerts and farmers' market on the village green, fireworks at Colgate at night.

"Town ball takes place in the late afternoon. Rich has two sets (maybe a dozen each) of old, scratchy baseball shirts—one striped, one tan—for the teams, chosen up at random, mostly men and boys but also some girls.

"Rich lays out the four stakes in a diamond shape, explains the rules (no gloves, no out of bounds, etc.). A local fellow serves as the referee in tails and a top hat. I can't ever remember his having to settle any dispute.

"The ball is soft. The pitching is overhand but not fast. The game is somewhat anarchic, from the perspective of baseball's rigidity. The ball can be hit, or nicked, in any direction, and it is in play. Runners don't have to run to any one stake. So, if you bat the ball toward the first stake, you can avoid being 'plugged' (there are lots of interesting bits of arcane vocabulary).

"Runners can also get away to avoid being plugged. So, this past year, we chased a young fellow into right field, aiming to plug him. We thought we had him cornered by Payne Creek, which runs across the outfield, where there was a children's toy boat race taking place. But the runner leapt into the creek, crossed to the other side, and taunted us from a safe distance. We returned to pitch to the next batter.

"While this little bit of anarchy was taking place, I'm sure the audience and most of the other players were finding the game a little dowdy, but we were having fun. We played a couple games this past year. I think we set the winning number of tallies at 20 or 25. Each game took about an hour at the most."

The image of my kid brother, cavorting on the national holiday, going back a century and a half, brings back immensely joyous memories of our backyard games. The sport still brings out the child in some of us. It started on lawns and that is where it will endure.

ACKNOWLEDGMENTS

My first debt is to the writers who have contributed to this lovely series. Their work and reputations made me want to be part of the team.

I wish to thank Julia Cheiffetz of Random House, who made this book twice as good as I would have done on my own. Also, thanks to Esther Newberg, my agent, who lets me see the Red Sox through her heart. And thanks to my wife, Marianne Graham Vecsey, for the advice that always works. I do listen to you.

I also want to thank Ted Spencer, the chief curator, and Jeff Idelson and Bill Francis of the National Baseball Hall of Fame and Museum, along with members of the Society of American Baseball Researchers (SABR), who have laid out an amazing amount of baseball history. And in particular, John Thorn, who was so generous with ideas, contacts, and information.

In no particular order, other kind people include:

Yoshi Demura, Brad Lefton, Dave Ornauer, Haruko Hasami, Bobby Valentine, Ken Belson, Bruce Picken, David Falkner, Yasumasa Ishikawa and our good friends, the Usuzaka family, for teaching me about Japan. Domo arigato.

Mark and Josephine Harris. Branch B. Rickey, for the stories about his grandfather. George Shuba, one of the Boys of Summer. Garrett Squires, nephew of Roger Connor. Abe J. Schear, for his enlightening interviews with baseball people.

David Block, who wrote an excellent book and then answered a lot of my questions. Fay Vincent. Peter Ueberroth. Ralph Branca. Buzzie Bavasi, a grand storyteller. Christopher Vecsey, Ph.D., my kid brother.

Karen D. Thompson, Information and Research Services Branch, Population Division, U.S. Census Bureau. Martina Bagnoli, Associate Curator, Manuscripts and Rare Books, Walters Art Museum, Baltimore, Maryland. Jeffrey Eric Jenkins, Department of Drama, Tisch School of the Arts, New York University, for his e-mail about Frazee and *Nanette.* Kate Salem, University of Nebraska Press.

Peter C. Bjarkman. Douglas Logan. Sandra Levinson, Center for Cuban Studies, New York. Bob Waterman of the Elias Sports Bureau. Stan Isaacs. Buck O'Neil, who taught us about the Negro Leagues, and then taught us about grace. The late Al Campanis, a good man who was so proud of Jackie, Campy, Newk, and Gilliam.

Glenn Stout, for his knowledge about Ruth, Frazee, and the Robinson tryout. Alan Taxerman, who gives me insight into the demanding world of the Yankee fan. And Ray Robinson, for his books, plus the long lunches, talking baseball—and politics.

And finally, my parents, George Vecsey and May Spencer Vecsey, journalists and union pioneers who made me want to go into the family trade.

BIBLIOGRAPHY

Ashe, Arthur R., Jr. *A Hard Road to Glory: Baseball: The African-American Athlete in Baseball.* New York: Amistad, 1988.

Asinof, Eliot. *Eight Men Out.* New York: Holt, Rinehart & Winston, 1963.

Astor, Gerald, editor. *National Baseball Hall of Fame and Museum: 50th Anniversary Book.* New York: Prentice Hall, 1988.

Block, David. *Baseball Before We Knew It: A Search for the Roots of the Game.* Lincoln: University of Nebraska Press, 2005.

Boswell, Thomas. *How Life Imitates the World Series.* Garden City: Doubleday, 1982.

Clark, Joe. *A History of Australian Baseball.* Lincoln: University of Nebraska Press, 2003.

Eig, Jonathan. *Luckiest Man: The Life and Death of Lou Gehrig.* New York: Simon & Schuster, 2005.

Fainaru-Wada, Mark, and Lance Williams. *Game of Shadows: Barry Bonds, BALCO, and the Steroids Scandal That Rocked Professional Sports.* New York: Gotham, 2006.

Fetter, Henry D. *Taking On the Yankees.* New York: W. W. Norton, 2003.

Flood, Curt, with Richard Carter. *The Way It Is.* New York: Pocket, 1972.

Goldstein, Richard. *Spartan Seasons: How Baseball Survived the Second World War.* New York: Macmillan, 1980.

Goldstein, Warren. *Playing for Keeps: A History of Early Baseball.* Ithaca: Cornell University Press, 1989.

González Echevarría, Roberto. *The Pride of Havana: A History of Cuban Baseball.* New York: Oxford University Press, 1999.

Harris, Mark. *The Southpaw.* Lincoln: University of Nebraska Press, 2003. (Orig. pub. 1953.)

Helyar, John. *Lords of the Realm: The Real History of Baseball.* New York: Villard, 1994.

Jensen, Don. *The Timeline History of Baseball.* New York: Palgrave Macmillan, 2005.

Koppett, Leonard. *Koppett's Concise History of Major League Baseball.* New York: Carroll & Graf, 2004.

Kuhn, Bowie. *Hardball: The Education of a Baseball Commissioner.* New York: Times Books, 1987.

Lamster, Mark. *Spalding's World Tour: The Epic Adventure That Took Baseball Around the Globe and Made It America's Game.* New York: Public Affairs, 2006.

Levine, Peter. *A. G. Spalding and the Rise of Baseball.* New York: Oxford University Press, 1985.

Mann, Jack. *The Decline and Fall of the New York Yankees.* New York: Simon & Schuster, 1967.

Maraniss, David. *Clemente: The Passion and Grace of Baseball's Last Hero.* New York: Simon & Schuster, 2006.

Miller, Marvin. *A Whole Different Ball Game.* Chicago: Ivan R. Dee, 2004.

Nuñez, Bernardo B., and Camilo A. Nuñez. *Su Majestad, El Baseball, Rey de los Deportes.* Panama: Playball Sports, 2002.

Obojski, Robert. *Bush League: A History of Minor League Baseball.* New York: Macmillan, 1975.

Oh, Sadaharu, with David Falkner. *A Zen Way of Baseball.* New York: Times Books, 1984.

Oleksak, Michael M., and Mary Adams Oleksak. *Beisbol: Latin Americans and the Grand Old Game.* Grand Rapids, Michigan: Masters Press, 1991.

Rampersad, Arnold. *Jackie Robinson: A Biography.* New York: Alfred A. Knopf, 1997.

Reaves, Joseph A. *Taking In a Game: A History of Baseball in Asia.* Lincoln: University of Nebraska Press, 2000.

Riley, James A. *The Biographical Encyclopedia of the Negro Baseball Leagues.* New York: Carroll & Graf, 1994.

Ritter, Lawrence. *The Glory of Their Times.* New expanded edition. New York: William Morrow, 1984.

Robinson, Jackie, as told to Alfred Duckett. *I Never Had It Made.* New York: G. P. Putnam's Sons, 1972.

Robinson, Ray. *Iron Horse: Lou Gehrig in His Prime.* New York: W. W. Norton, 2006. (Orig. pub. 1990.)

————. *Matty: An American Hero.* New York: Oxford University Press, 1993.

Rogosin, Donn. *Invisible Men.* New York: Atheneum, 1983.

Ryan, Bob. *When Boston Won the World Series.* Philadelphia: Running Press, 2002.

Shapiro, Michael. *The Last Good Season.* New York: Doubleday, 2003.

Smelser, Marshall. *The Life That Ruth Built.* Lincoln: University of Nebraska Press, 1993.

Smith, Curt. *Voices of Summer: Ranking Baseball's 101 All-Time Best Announcers.* New York: Carroll & Graf, 2005.

————. *Voices of the Game.* New York: Simon & Schuster, 1987.

Stout, Glenn. *Yankees Century: 100 Years of New York Yankees Baseball.* New York: Houghton Mifflin, 2002.

Sullivan, Neil. *The Diamond in the Rough: Yankee Stadium and the Politics of New York.* New York: Oxford University Press, 2001.

Thorn, John, with Pete Palmer, Michael Gershman, and David Pietrusza. *Total Baseball: The Official Encyclopedia of Major League Baseball.* Sixth Edition. New York: Total Sports, 1999.

Tygiel, Jules. *Baseball as History.* New York: Oxford University Press, 2000.

Whiting, Robert. *The Chrysanthemum and the Bat: Baseball Samurai Style.* New York: Dodd, Mead, 1977.

NOTES

I: SIX DEGREES

3 Musial in Japan: Lee Kavetski, "Stan 'the Man' Musial—A Class Guy," *Stars and Stripes,* January 24, 1988.

3 Oh and Musial crouch: Sadaharu Oh, with David Falkner, *A Zen Way of Baseball* (New York: Times Books, 1984), p. 81.

9 Merkle and 1908: Lawrence Ritter, *The Glory of Their Times,* new expanded edition (New York: William Morrow, 1984), pp. 105–8.

10 legacy of the game: Tom Shieber and Ted Spencer, *Baseball as America: Seeing Ourselves Through Our National Game.* Washington, D.C.: National Geographic, 2002.

11 "Take Me Out to the Ball Game": Baseball-Almanac.com.

11 Tagliabue and baseball: Karl Taro Greenfeld, "The Big Man," *Sports Illustrated,* January 23, 2006.

12 "Casey at the Bat": Favoritepoem.org.

12 "I went back": Mark Harris, *The Southpaw* (Lincoln: University of Nebraska Press, 2003), pp. 287–88.

II: BERBERS WITH BATS

17 blond Berbers: David Block, *Baseball Before We Knew It: A Search for the Roots of the Game* (Lincoln: University of Nebraska Press, 2005), pp. 95–99.

18 Spanish drawing: Bill Pennington, "They Ain't Found Till They're Found," *New York Times,* September 12, 2004.

18 Flanders ball: Block, *Baseball Before We Knew It,* p. 148.

18 Stow and London: Ibid., pp. 166–67.

19 Newbery and baseball: Ibid., pp. 178–79.

19 Gutsmuths: Ibid., pp. 67–73.

20 Silesian glass-blowers: Ibid., p. 101.

20 The game that flourished: *National Baseball Hall of Fame and Museum: 50th Anniversary Book,* edited by Gerald Astor (New York: Prentice Hall, 1988), pp. 1–4.

20 Doc Adams: John Thorn, "The True Father of Baseball," *Elysian Fields Quarterly,* Winter 1992.

23 first admissions: John Odell, "Curator's Corner: The All-Stars Are Not the Only All-Stars," *Memories and Dreams* (Baseball Hall of Fame quarterly magazine), Spring 2003.

23 James Creighton: Leonard Koppett, *Koppett's Concise History of Major League Baseball* (New York: Carroll & Graf, 2004), p. 46.

24 Creighton death: John Thorn, SABR Baseball Biography Project.

24 Cuthbert and stolen bases: Don Jensen, *The Timeline History of Baseball* (New York: Palgrave Macmillan, 2005).

25 U.S. Grant and Red Stockings: Harvey Frommer, "The Birth of Baseball's First Professional Team," Frommer Sportsnet, 2005.

III: THE FIRST ENTREPRENEUR

29 Spalding and "manliness": Peter Levine, *A. G. Spalding and the Rise of Baseball* (New York: Oxford University Press, 1985), p. 119.

29 Spalding and professionalism: Ibid., p. 14.

30 Spalding as entrepreneur: Ibid., p. 44.

30 Spalding's awareness of thèque: David Block, *Baseball Before We Knew It: A Search for the Roots of the Game* (Lincoln: University of Nebraska Press, 2005), p. 11.

30 Chadwick and *Beadle's*: Levine, *A. G. Spalding and the Rise of Baseball,* p. 19.

31 "Boston is in mourning": Ibid., p. 21.

32 Spalding and sporting goods: Leonard Koppett, *Koppett's Concise History of Major League Baseball* (New York: Carroll & Graf, 2004).

32 Chadwick and the K: Jules Tygiel, *Baseball as History* (New York: Oxford University Press, 2000), p. 23.

32 Salary cap: Koppett, *Koppett's Concise History of Major League Baseball,* p. 57.

32 Spalding and Chadwick and labor: Levine, *A. G. Spalding and the Rise of Baseball,* p. 53.

32 Australia trip: John Rossi, "The Great Base Ball Trip Around the World in 1888–89," LaSalle University in Philadelphia, Nationalpastime.com.

33 Duval and leash: Mark Lamster, *Spalding's World Tour: The Epic Adventure That Took Baseball Around the Globe and Made It America's Game* (New York: Public Affairs, 2006), p. 317.

33 Twain at Delmonico's: *Boston Daily Globe,* April 9, 1889.

33 Delmonico's menu: Lamster, *Spalding's World Tour,* p. xv.

34 Louisville scandal: Eliot Asinof, *Eight Men Out* (New York: Holt, Rinehart & Winston, 1963), pp. 11–12.

34 Comiskey and playing wide: Tygiel, *Baseball as History,* p. 43.

35 Roger Connor: Mike Attiyeh, "Roger Connor: The 19th Century HR King," baseballguru.com.

35 "The family old-timers": E-mail from Garrett Squires, Connor's grandnephew, February 5, 2005.

36 Anson and Ward at Delmonico's: *New York Times,* April 9, 1889.

37 Mack and the Brotherhood: Tygiel, *Baseball as History,* p. 45.

38 Philadelphia Pythians: Don Jensen, *The Timeline History of Baseball* (New York: Palgrave Macmillan, 2005).

38 Bud Fowler and Page Fence Giants: Ibid.

38 Moses Fleetwood Walker: Arthur R. Ashe, Jr., *A Hard Road to Glory: Baseball: The African-American Athlete in Baseball* (New York: Amistad, 1988), pp. 3–4.

38 Anson and Stovey: Michael M. Oleksak and Mary Adams Oleksak, *Beisbol: Latin Americans and the Grand Old Game* (Grand Rapids, Michigan: Masters Press, 1991), p. 26.

IV: COLUMBUS, POCAHONTAS, AND DOUBLEDAY

41 Doubleday: Richard J. Tofel, "Regarding the 'Innocuous Conspiracy' of Baseball's Birth: Two Long-Lost Letters Show How Doubleday Was Credited with the Game's Invention," *Wall Street Journal,* July 19, 2001.

42 "an American Dad": Letter from Spalding to Murnane, January 25, 1905, courtesy of Bill Francis, researcher, National Baseball Hall of Fame Library, 2006.

42 Spalding resists Chadwick's rounders theory: Peter Levine, *A. G. Spalding and the Rise of Baseball* (New York: Oxford University Press, 1985), p. 113.

43 Graves letters: Courtesy of Ted Spencer, chief curator, National Baseball Hall of Fame and Museum, 2006.

43 no record of Doubleday visiting Cooperstown: Ted Spencer, chief

curator, National Baseball Hall of Fame and Museum, e-mail, February 16, 2006.

43 Doubleday never wrote about baseball: Victor Salvatore, "The Man Who Didn't Invent Baseball," *American Heritage,* June/July 1983.

43 "You ask for some information": Letter to unknown correspondent, November 20, 1887, courtesy National Baseball Hall of Fame Library, 2006.

44 Abner Demas Doubleday: David Block, *Baseball Before We Knew It: A Search for the Roots of the Game* (Lincoln: University of Nebraska Press, 2005), p. 58.

44 Mills in honor guard for Doubleday: Levine, *A. G. Spalding and the Rise of Baseball,* p. 114.

47 Alexander and Hall: *Sporting News,* January 27, 1938, p. 4.

47 Ted Williams and Negro League stars: Donn Rogosin, *Invisible Men* (New York: Atheneum, 1983), p. 176.

V: GROWING PAINS

51 Ban Johnson and Western League: Eliot Asinof, *Eight Men Out* (New York: Holt, Rinehart & Winston, 1963), p. 75.

52 Athletics "white elephants": Leonard Koppett, *Koppett's Concise History of Major League Baseball* (New York: Carroll & Graf, 2004), p. 95.

53 crowds in Boston: Bob Ryan, *When Boston Won the World Series* (Philadelphia: Running Press, 2002), p. 100.

53 "Tessie": Ibid., p. 135.

53 Mathewson and Sunday: Ray Robinson, *Matty: An American Hero* (New York: Oxford University Press, 1993), p. 12.

54 Eddie Grant, Argonne Forest: Ibid., p. 186.

55 Federal League and Mack: Jules Tygiel, *Baseball as History* (New York: Oxford University Press, 2000), p. 59.

56 Landis "shocked": Rick Burton, "From Hearst to Stern: The Shaping of an Industry Over a Century," *New York Times,* December 19, 1999.

VI: THE BLACK SOX

60 Hal Chase and $50: Eliot Asinof, *Eight Men Out* (New York: Holt, Rinehart & Winston, 1963), p. 14.

60 White Sox salaries: Ibid., pp. 17–18.

61 Cicotte hits Rath: Ibid., pp. 64–65.

62 "whelp of a beaten cur": Ibid., p. 77.

63 push for a neutral leader: Leonard Koppett, *Koppett's Concise History of Major League Baseball* (New York: Carroll & Graf, 2004), p. 135.

64 "Birds of a feather": Asinof, *Eight Men Out*, p. 280.

64 Cobb and Speaker: Koppett, *Koppett's Concise History of Major League Baseball*, p. 164.

VII: THE BABE

68 father never visited St. Mary's school: Marshall Smelser, *The Life That Ruth Built* (Lincoln: University of Nebraska Press, 1993), p. 11.

68 Brother Matthias: Ibid., p. 14.

68 Dunn guardian: Ibid., p. 32.

68 "Jack Dunn's babes": Ibid., p. 39.

69 Ruppert and Huston: Ibid., p. 123.

69 Ruth $125,000 plus loan: Ibid., p. 128.

69 livelier baseballs: Leonard Koppett, *Koppett's Concise History of Major League Baseball* (New York: Carroll & Graf, 2004), p. 139.

70 better wool: Smelser, *The Life That Ruth Built*, p. 189.

70 "The House That Ruth Built": Ibid., p. 274.

71 Gehrig's farewell speech: Jonathan Eig, *Luckiest Man: The Life and Death of Lou Gehrig* (New York: Simon & Schuster, 2005), p. 317.

73 Henry Ford: Glenn Stout, *Yankees Century: 100 Years of New York Yankees Baseball* (New York: Houghton Mifflin, 2002).

73 anti-Semitic material: "Jewish Degradation of American Baseball," *Dearborn Independent,* September 10, 1921; Glenn Stout, "Nothing but the Truth: The Untold History of the 'Curse,' " *Elysian Fields Quarterly,* Fall 2005.

74 Frazee estate: Stout, *Yankees Century.*

VIII: MR. RICKEY

77 Rickey stolen bases: Mark Herrmann, "Branch Rickey: One Man's Vision Changed Baseball Forever," *Newsday,* March 16, 1997.

79 Knothole Gang: Mike Eisenbath, "Branch Took the Birds, and Baseball, Out of the Woods," *St. Louis Post-Dispatch,* May 5, 1992.

79 Cardinals impoverished: Henry D. Fetter, *Taking On the Yankees* (New York: W. W. Norton, 2003), p. 108.

79 "the king of the weeds": Ibid., p. 119.

79 "lending" players: Ibid., p. 122.

80 Holmes on reserve clause: Allen Guttmann, "When Supreme Court Rules," *New York Times,* September 9, 1984.

80 "sport, not trade": John Helyar, *Lords of the Realm: The Real History of Baseball* (New York: Villard, 1994), p. 10.

80 fifty ex-farmhands in majors: Ibid., p. 173.

80 "South Dakota, North Dakota": Interview with Branch B. Rickey, 2005.

81 Schoendienst and CCC: BaseballLibrary.com.

81 Slaughter and hunting dogs: Interview with Branch B. Rickey, 2005.

81 Giants, Yankees resist farm system: Fetter, *Taking On the Yankees,* p. 154.

81 Yanks emulated Cardinals: Marshall Smelser, *The Life That Ruth Built* (Lincoln: University of Nebraska Press, 1993), p. 405.

81 Newark farm team: Fetter, *Taking On the Yankees,* p. 104.

IX: THE NEGRO LEAGUES

87 some Cubans not white: Roberto González Echevarría, *The Pride of Havana: A History of Cuban Baseball* (New York: Oxford University Press, 1999), p. 255.

88 "Cherokee" bellhop: Arthur R. Ashe, Jr., *A Hard Road to Glory: Baseball: The African-American Athlete in Baseball* (New York: Amistad, 1988), p. 15.

88 Ban Johnson bans white players: Ibid., p. 18.

88 "no makeshift club": Michael M. Oleksak and Mary Adams Oleksak, *Beisbol: Latin Americans and the Grand Old Game* (Grand Rapids, Michigan: Masters Press, 1991), p. 22.

89 Andrew (Rube) Foster: Ashe, *A Hard Road to Glory,* pp. 17, 23.

89 Foster rebuilds grandstand: Donn Rogosin, *Invisible Men* (New York: Atheneum, 1983), p. 8.

89 Foster and black owners: Jules Tygiel, *Baseball as History* (New York: Oxford University Press, 2000), p. 116.

89 Landis forbids major league uniforms: John B. Holway, "A Vote for Chandler, an Ignored Pioneer," *New York Times,* March 1, 1981.

89 Homestead Grays and Posey: Negroleaguebaseball.com.

90 Greenlee buys Crawfords: Rogosin, *Invisible Men,* p. 15.

90 five Hall of Famers on Crawfords: Ibid., p. 17.

90 Gibson joins Grays, 1930: Ibid., p. 53.

90 baseball as black industry: Ibid., p. 6.

91 nine consecutive championships: Negroleaguebaseball.com.

92 "shadow ball": *Baseball,* documentary by Ken Burns, 1994.

92 Dean praises Paige: Rogosin, *Invisible Men,* p. 124.

92 Negro League victories: Burns, *Baseball*.

92 "In games between": Jules Tygiel, "The Negro Leagues," *Organization of American Historians, Magazine of History*, Summer 1992.

92 innovations by Bassett, Wells: Rogosin, *Invisible Men*, p. 74.

92 Manley and Newark Eagles: National Baseball Hall of Fame and Museum, 2006.

93 Willie Wells in Mexico: Wendell Smith, *Pittsburgh Courier*, May 6, 1944.

93 bridge named for Grays: Associated Press, "Bridge Name Honors Homestead Grays," July 14, 2002.

93 Negro League merchandise: Richard Sandomir, "Survivors of Negro League Reaping the Benefits," *New York Times*, February 12, 1995.

x: RADIO DAYS

97 converted telephone: Curt Smith, *Voices of the Game* (New York: Simon & Schuster, 1987), p. 6.

97 "I was just a nobody": Ibid., p. 7.

97 first World Series broadcast: Stan Isaacs, "Baseball's Radio Pioneers," *Newsday*, July 11, 1989.

98 "I don't know which": Smith, *Voices of the Game*, p. 12.

98 "rough around the edges": Ibid., p. 20.

99 "Aunt Minnie": Ibid., p. 76.

99 Barber and "Arabian horse": Gerald Ensley, "Red Barber's Career Marked by Pride, Accuracy and Integrity," Knight-Ridder, October 25, 1992.

100 "good and dark": Jerome Holtzman, "An Enlightening Journey Through Night-Game Annals," *Chicago Tribune*, August 8, 1988.

101 Joe Bowman: Les Bowen, "Wrigley Field Sees the Light," *Philadelphia Inquirer*, August 8, 1988.

101 percentage of night games: Telephone interview with Bob Waterman, Elias Sports Bureau, 2005.

102 "The Rembrandt of Re-creation": Isaacs, "Baseball's Radio Pioneers."

102 Barbar, NBC, 1939: Smith, *Voices of the Game*, p. 40.

106 first peacetime draft: Richard Goldstein, *Spartan Seasons: How Baseball Survived the Second World War* (New York: Macmillan, 1980), p. 3.

xi: WAR

109 sign of weakness: Richard Goldstein, *Spartan Seasons: How Baseball Survived the Second World War* (New York: Macmillan, 1980), p. 37.

109 "green light" letter: Ibid., p. 19.

110   over 100 major-leaguers in uniform: Leonard Koppett, *Koppett's Concise History of Major League Baseball* (New York: Carroll & Graf, 2004), p. 212.

110   Chandler and baseball: Goldstein, *Spartan Seasons,* p. 202.

111   Moreland and Mexico: Jules Tygiel, *Baseball as History* (New York: Oxford University Press, 2000).

112   Gedeon and O'Neill: Goldstein, *Spartan Seasons,* p. 249.

112   Bert Shepard: Ibid., pp. 212–13.

113   Harry Walker: Ibid., p. 252.

114   Pesky and DiMaggio: telephone interviews with George Vecsey, October 17, 2002.

115   O'Doul in Japan: Lawrence Ritter, *The Glory of Their Times* (New York: William Morrow, 1984), p. 278.

115   MacArthur and O'Doul: Japanese ambassador to the United States, Ryozo Kato, speech, Washington, D.C., January 17, 2006.

XII: JACKIE ROBINSON

119   "snowflake": Jackie Robinson, as told to Alfred Duckett, *I Never Had It Made* (New York: G. P. Putnam's Sons, 1972), p. 63.

120   Robinson and newspapers: Interview with Jackie Robinson by George Vecsey, *Newsday,* 1967.

120   Lester Rodney: Jack Epstein, "Baseball's Conscience Finally Gets His Due," *San Francisco Chronicle,* July 10, 2005.

121   Dykes and tryout: John B. Holway, "A Vote for Chandler, an Ignored Pioneer, *New York Times,* March 1, 1981.

121   "on his lips": John B. Holway, "A Vote for Chandler, an Ignored Pioneer," *New York Times,* March 1, 1981.

121   "my predecessor": Joseph Durso, "Aaron, Robinson Inducted and Honored as Pioneers," *New York Times,* August 2, 1982.

121   Robinson in Boston: Glenn Stout, "Tryout and Fallout: Race, Jackie Robinson and the Red Sox," *Massachusetts Historical Review,* Volume 6, 2004.

122   Charles Thomas: James A. Riley, *The Biographical Encyclopedia of the Negro Baseball Leagues* (New York: Carroll & Graf, 1994), pp. 121–22.

122   "guts enough not to fight back": Arnold Rampersad, *Jackie Robinson: A Biography* (New York: Alfred A. Knopf, 1997), p. 126.

122   "vindictive spikes": Ibid., p. 127.

123   Cardinal boycott threat: Harold Rosenthal, "The Story Behind the Story," *New York Times,* May 4, 1997.

124 Sisler and Robinson: Rampersad, *Jackie Robinson,* p. 208.
124 Shuba anecdote: Letter to George Vecsey, circa 1982.

XIII: BASEBALL HITS THE INTERSTATE

132 Veeck and Phillies: John B. Holway, "A Vote for Chandler, an Ignored Pioneer," *New York Times,* March 1, 1981.
132 Veeck and attendance: John Helyar, *Lords of the Realm: The Real History of Baseball* (New York: Villard, 1994), p. 235.
133 Veeck and television: Jules Tygiel, *Baseball as History* (New York: Oxford University Press, 2000), p. 155.
133 attendance figures: Ibid., p. 303.
134 Dodger television revenue: Henry D. Fetter, *Taking On the Yankees* (New York: W. W. Norton, 2003), p. 230.

XIV: FREE AGENCY ARRIVES

141 Flood background: Thomas Boswell, *How Life Imitates the World Series* (Garden City: Doubleday, 1982).
141 union history: Major League Baseball Players Association, MLBPlayers.com.
142 "deep hatred and suspicion": Bowie Kuhn, *Hardball: The Education of a Baseball Commissioner* (New York: Times Books, 1987), p. 77.
142 "aberration, a temporary irritation": Marvin Miller, *A Whole Different Ball Game* (Chicago: Ivan R. Dee, 2004), p. 91.
143 $1,000 raise in twenty years: John Helyar, *Lords of the Realm: The Real History of Baseball* (New York: Villard, 1994), p. 10.
143 "slaves and pieces of property": Murray Chass, "A World of Change in the Money Game," *New York Times,* December 30, 1979.
144 Flood trial: Joseph Durso, "Curt Flood Is Dead at 59," *New York Times,* January 21, 1997.
144 Flood's childhood friend: Curt Flood, with Richard Carter, *The Way It Is* (New York: Pocket, 1972).
144 Garagiola on Flood: Murray Chass, "Flood Was a Man for Every Season," *New York Times,* January 21, 1997.
145 "I don't think": Miller, *A Whole Different Ball Game,* p. 194.
145 Thurgood Marshall dissent: *Flood v. Kuhn,* 407 U.S. 258 (1972), laws.findlaw.com/us/407/258.html.
145 "I did a double take": Miller, *A Whole Different Ball Game,* p. 41.
145 no tax deduction for Finley: Helyar, *Lords of the Realm,* p. 137.
146 Hunter and free agency: Ibid., p. 140.

146 "before the ink was dry": Miller, *A Whole Different Ball Game,* p. 251.

146 payroll increases: Helyar, *Lords of the Realm,* p. 349.

146 "anti-management bias": Kuhn, *Hardball,* p. 157.

146 cable television revenue: Helyar, *Lords of the Realm,* p. 372.

147 strike insurance ran out: Koppett, *Koppett's Concise History of Major League Baseball,* p. 391.

147 salaries, 1976–1985: Miller, *A Whole Different Ball Game,* pp. 286, 318.

147 salaries, 1989–1991: Helyar, *Lords of the Realm,* p. 455.

147 "Mickey Mantle made $100,000": Murray Chass, "A World of Change in the Money Game," *New York Times,* December 30, 1979.

147 Boras: Tom Verducci, "Big Deals," *Sports Illustrated,* June 14, 1993.

147 "first ballplayer who made sacrifices": Joseph Durso, "Aaron, Robinson Inducted and Honored as Pioneers," *New York Times,* August 2, 1982.

148 Flood on free agency: Steve Jacobson, "His Fight for Freedom Cost Him Dearly," *Newsday,* January 21, 1997.

148 1997 salaries: Murray Chass, "Believe It or Not: Steinbrenner Is Being Outspent," *New York Times,* April 2, 1998.

XV: WHY THE YANKEES EXIST

152 Ruppert management: Henry D. Fetter, *Taking On the Yankees* (New York: W. W. Norton, 2003), p. 9.

153 Yankee–Kansas City transactions: John Thorn, with Pete Palmer, Michael Gershman, and David Pietrusza, *Total Baseball: The Official Encyclopedia of Major League Baseball,* Sixth Edition (New York: Macmillan, 1999), pp. 2371–2579.

154 Yankee attendance: Fetter, *Taking On the Yankees,* p. 8.

155 sale to CBS: Ibid.

156 three firings: Jack Mann, *The Decline and Fall of the New York Yankees* (New York: Simon & Schuster, 1967), pp. 205–17.

158 value of Yankees: Richard Sandomir, "Big Spending by Yankees Is Not Proof of Big Profits," *New York Times,* January 6, 2005; Fetter, *Taking On the Yankees,* p. 304.

159 Yankees worth $1.026 billion: Michael K. Ozanian and Lesley Kump, "Steinbrenner's Tax Shelter," *Forbes,* May 8, 2006.

159 Manfred rebuts *Forbes*: "MLB Objects to *Forbes*' Estimates," Associated Press, April 22, 2006.

XVI: THE WORLD CATCHES UP

163 baseball in China: Joseph A. Reaves, *Taking In a Game: A History of Baseball in Asia* (Lincoln: University of Nebraska Press, 2000), pp. 14–16, via faroutliers.blogspot.com/2004.

163 Wilson and Hiraoka: Ibid.

164 first game in Japan: Akio Nikaido, in *Mainichi Shimbun,* May 7, 2000, citing research by Masanori Hirota, posted by Robert Whiting on faroutliers.blogspot.com.

164 O'Doul and Japan: Lawrence Ritter, *The Glory of Their Times* (New York: William Morrow, 1984), pp. 276–78.

165 Arakawa and Oh: Sadaharu Oh, with David Falkner, *A Zen Way of Baseball* (New York: Times Books, 1984), pp. 81, 111–35.

166 "never really friends": Ibid., p. 75.

166 Oh and Nagashima: Robert Whiting, *The Chrysanthemum and the Bat: Baseball Samurai Style* (New York: Dodd, Mead, 1977), p. 110.

169 "coffee-colored Cubans": Michael M. Oleksak and Mary Adams Oleksak, *Beisbol: Latin Americans and the Grand Old Game* (Grand Rapids, Michigan: Masters Press, 1991), p. 22.

169 record of 32-32-1: Ibid., p. 23.

169 "olive-skinned": Ibid., p. 26.

169 Luque and "Mardy": Sal Maglie with Dick Schaap, "I Always Threw Bean Balls," *Cavalier,* September 1959.

170 Minoso family name: Ibid., p. 56.

171 Clemente hidden: Jack Mann, *The Decline and Fall of the New York Yankees* (New York: Simon & Schuster, 1967), p. 17.

171 Clemente's No. 21: Interviews with Roberto Clemente, Jr., and Luis Clemente, March 2006.

172 Ichiro: Timothy Egan, "As Suzuki Chased History, the Hits Just Kept On Coming," *New York Times,* October 3, 2004.

172 Sisler: John McGrath, "Sisler Reheated," *Tacoma News Tribune,* September 2, 2004.

173 "If my grandfather": Art Thiel, "Ichiro Fashions Link to Baseball's Immortals," *Seattle Post-Intelligencer,* October 2, 2004.

173 "so little time": Larry Larue, "The Hit King," *Tacoma News Tribune,* October 2, 2004.

173 Rangers bow to Ichiro: Ibid.

173 international baseball: Interview with Sadaharu Oh, January 17, 2006, Washington, D.C.

174 Antonio Castro: Jack Curry, "Son of Fidel Castro Is Making a Name for Himself with Cuba's Team," *New York Times,* March 9, 2006.

XVII: SAME GAME, YUPPIFIED

178 innovations (unless otherwise noted): Don Jensen, *The Timeline History of Baseball* (New York: Palgrave Macmillan, 2005).

178 "When we arrived in Jacksonville": Brian Schmitz, "A Swing Through Spring Training," *Orlando Sentinel,* February 23, 2003.

179 Bresnahan batting helmet: Kate Ledger, "Safety Did Not Come First Even After a Fatal 1920 Beaning," *Sports Illustrated,* July 14, 1997.

179 the Babe's trainer: Marshall Smelser, *The Life That Ruth Built* (Lincoln: University of Nebraska Press, 1993), pp. 326–28.

179 amplifier: Leonard Koppett, *Koppett's Concise History of Major League Baseball* (New York: Carroll & Graf, 2004), p. 186.

179 uniform numbers: Smelser, *The Life That Ruth Built,* p. 391.

180 Pirates wear helmets: Ledger, "Safety Did Not Come First Even After a Fatal 1920 Beaning."

180 Veeck proposed interleague play: Koppett, *Koppett's Concise History of Major League Baseball,* p. 487.

180 bad-taste uniforms: Patricia Leigh Brown, "The Champions and Cellar-Dwellers of Fashion," *New York Times,* July 18, 1993.

182 "Marberry as an intimidator": Shirley Povich, "Baseball No Longer Speaks Same Language," *Washington Post,* March 20, 1996.

186 SkyDome: John Helyar, *Lords of the Realm: The Real History of Baseball* (New York: Villard, 1994) p. 447.

XVIII: WHO'S IN CHARGE?

Source of information in this chapter, unless otherwise noted: National Baseball Hall of Fame and Museum yearbook.

191 "Well argued": Richard Goldstein, "Wellington Mara, Patriarch of N.F.L., Dies at 89," *New York Times,* October 26, 2005.

196 Ueberroth tried to force centralization: Ibid., p. 407.

196 Giamatti and Rose: Ibid., p. 408.

XIX: FOUR SCANDALS

202 "like jelly beans": Lee Jenkins with Juliet Macur and Bill Pennington, "A Chance for Baseball to Settle Its Drug Score," *New York Times,* December 12, 2004.

202 Hernandez testimony: Associated Press, "Met Testifies of 'Romance' Between Players and Drugs," September 6, 1985.

203 collusion and 1985 Collective Bargaining Agreement: Leonard Koppett, *Koppett's Concise History of Major League Baseball* (New York: Carroll & Graf, 2004), p. 415.

203 Dawson salary: Murray Chass, "Baseball: Big Collusion Winners: Clark, Parrish, Dawson," *New York Times,* December 15, 1992.

204 Settlement for $280 million: Richard Sandomir, "Players Association Priority: Taking Care of Business, *New York Times,* August 11, 1991.

204 Curt Flood Act: "Antitrust Exemption Is Partly Revoked," Associated Press, *New York Times,* October 28, 1998.

205 Rose at World Series: Richard Sandomir, "All-Century Became All About Rose and Gray," *New York Times,* October 31, 1999.

206 "Charles Manson": George Vecsey, "The All-Century Player Who Haunts Baseball," *New York Times,* October 25, 1999.

206 home runs and labor stoppage: Koppett, *Koppett's Concise History of Major League Baseball,* p. 481.

208 Bonds and steroids: Lance Williams and Mark Fainaru-Wada, "What Bonds Told BALCO Grand Jury," *San Francisco Chronicle,* December 3, 2004.

XX: OCTOBER EXORCISMS

219 Pesky interview: George Vecsey, Fenway Park, October 2004.

EPILOGUE

221 e-mail: Christopher Vecsey, Ph.D., Colgate University.

INDEX

About the Author

GEORGE VECSEY, a sports columnist for *The New York Times*, has written about such events as the FIFA World Cup and the Olympics but considers baseball, the sport he's covered since 1960, his favorite game. He is the author of more than a dozen books, including *Loretta Lynn: Coal Miner's Daughter* (with Loretta Lynn), which was made into an Academy Award–winning film. He has also served as national and religion reporter for *The New York Times*, interviewing the Dalai Lama, Tony Blair, Billy Graham, and a host of other noteworthy figures. He lives in New York with his wife, an artist.

A Note on the Type

The principal text of this Modern Library edition
was set in a digitized version of Janson, a typeface that
dates from about 1690 and was cut by Nicholas Kis,
a Hungarian working in Amsterdam. The original matrices have
survived and are held by the Stempel foundry in Germany.
Hermann Zapf redesigned some of the weights and sizes for
Stempel, basing his revisions on the original design.